The Future Master Fard Muhammad

By

The Most Hon. Elijah Muhammad

All Rights Reserved. No part of this book may be reproduced or transmitted in any form by any means, electronic, photocopying, mechanical, recording, information storage or retrieval system without permission from the publisher, The New World Nation of Islam. Brief quotations may be used in reviews or commentary.

The New World Nation of Islam
PO Box 8466
Newark, New Jersey 07108
973-678-9975
www.newworldnationislam.com
email: secretary@newworldnationislam.com

Copyright 2013 © by The New World Nation of Islam

The Future Master Fard Muhammad
ISBN 13-digit 978-0-9890425-0-5

Library of Congress Catalog Number
1. Elijah Muhammad, Black Muslims, Nation of Islam, Islam, Islam in North America, New World Nation of Islam, Muslims, F.O.I., M.G.T & G.C.C.

Cover design by Nuance Art .*.nuanceart@gmail.com
Interior book design by Nuance Art .*.nuanceart@gmail.com
Editorial Team: Nobel Ali, Samataha Ali, Kalimah Ali

Printed in United States
Green & Company Printing and Publishing, LLC
www.greenandcompany.biz

THE FUTURE MASTER FARD MUHAMMAD

BY

THE HONORABLE ELIJAH MUHAMAD

A NEW WORLD NATION OF ISLAM PUBLICATION

DEDICATON

This book is dedicated to The Honorable Mr. Elijah Muhammad. The Last God of the Old World and the First God of the New World Nation of Islam

ACKNOWLEDGEMENTS

We wish to thank the Mighty F.O.I. who participated in the research of the material of this book.

Bro. National Spokesman Mumin Allah

Bro. Field Major Aziz Allah

Bro. Field Major Samad Allah

Bro. Field Major Hadid Allah

Bro. Field Major Hakim Allah

Bro. Field Major Rahman Allah

Bro. Field Major Omar Allah

Bro. Field Major Rahim Allah

Bro. Field Major Jamil Allah

Bro. Field Major Hakim M. Allah

Bro. Field Major Basim Allah

Bro. Minister Najm Ali

Bro. Minister Khabir Ali

Bro. Minister Sabir Ali

Bro. Minister Razzaq Ali

Field Supreme Captain Mutadirah Wahida Ali, CEO of The New World Nation of Islam Publications

National Spokesman Mu-min Ali, Chief Editor

All questions and comments welcome! Direct any questions to: spokesman@newworldnationislam.com
FOI@newworldnationislam.com
MGT@newworldnationislam.com
Peace! Peace!

TABLE OF CONTENTS

Part I
Message To The Blackman 1

Part II
The Fall of America 25

Part III
Our Saviour Has Arrived 75

Part IV
How To Eat To Live 1 109

Part V
The Theology of Time 114

Part VI
The True History of Elijah Muhammad 134

Part VII
The Exegesis of the Pilgrimage 147

Part VIII
The Mother Plane 159

In the name of Allah, the Beneficent, the Merciful. We bear witness that Muhammad of 1400 years ago (PBUH) is Allah's last prophet. Peace, Peace.

INTRODUCTION

I am Field Supreme Minister, Ali Mahdi Muhammad. Spiritual leader of the New World Nation of Islam. The Field Supreme Staff was commissioned Saviour's Day, February 26, 1960.

That was the same day that our Father, the Most Honorable Elijah Muhammad told tens of thousands of His followers and announced to the world that He, Elijah was Allah, God.

He, Elijah said, "I have been made equal in knowledge with Allah. I control the winds and the seas. I have power over the sun, moon and stars. I have waited 379 years for this day."

The commissioning of the Field Supreme Staff was witnessed by twenty of the Nation of Islam's Ministers at the Minister's Meeting that day-Saviour's Day, 1960.

When Elijah (My God) said He is equal to Allah many people walked out of the auditorium. But we, the Field Staff believed every word he said. He began to teach us the secrets of God being among us and what we must do to build the House of Our Father's Desires. *(1 Chronicles 28:5-15)*

We, the New World Nation of Islam, are the original followers of the Honorable Elijah Muhammad. We are that infant nation, a nation within a nation, born to build a New World.

When our Father, the Honorable Elijah Muhammad, told us, the Field Staff that, "When you see Me, you see Allah, and when you see Allah, you see Me." We believed every word that came out of His mouth.

He, Elijah (My God) told us, the Field Supreme Staff that when the time is right, we will have to produce two books. One is for the Muslims and one of for the general public. The first book for the Muslims are a collection of the Teachings of our Father, the presence of God and the devil; The knowledge of the lost tribe of Shabazz, the God tribe, who are destined to inherit the earth and **The Future Master Fard Muhammad**. The second book is for the public, Uncle Yah Yah, 21st Century Man of Wisdom. It reveals that there is no god outside of man and no man outside of God.

The Honorable Elijah Muhammad told us that the reason that the Bible and Holy Qur'an predict that when the end comes, the New World Nation of Islam will be so little that they could only describe it (New World) as an infant or a baby nation. He said that is because we would only be a few followers. He said, "We will be lucky if we have a hand full when the end time comes." (*Holy Qur'an Chapter 19, Jesus Speaks from the Cradle and Bible Revelations Chapter 12, The Messenger Giving Birth to a Baby Nation*). The Honorable Elijah Muhammad is the Last God of the Old World and the First God of the New World.

My beloved black brothers and sisters, it is time to wake up. Stop looking for the Master Fard Muhammad of the past.

The secret is that you must look to **The Future Master Fard Muhammad** and His true identity is none other than Me and You.

May Allah bless us all. Peace to you in this world and peace to you in the Hereafter.

Your Brother,

Ali Mahdi Muhammad

PREFACE

In the name of Allah, the Beneficent, the Most Merciful, in the Person of Our Father, the Most Honorable Mr. Elijah Muhammad, Peace and Blessings of Allah be Upon Him Forever. And We Thank Master Fard Muhammad, Who came in the Person of Allah, in the year of 1930. He is the Manifestation of Almighty God, Allah. We will remember Him and Praise Him Forever and we will Honor Him by naming our children after Him for at least one thousand years. And we thank Our Father, the Most Honorable Mr. Elijah Muhammad for raising our Leader and Teacher of the New World Nation of Islam, Ali Mahdi Muhammad.

THE KEY

The Key to understanding the Teachings of Our Father, the Most Honorable Mr. Elijah Muhammad, is to know that the Most Honorable Mr. Elijah Muhammad says what He means and means what He says. Nothing is wrong. Everything is in time and on time, all the time. The history is already written, in twenty-five thousand year cycles. Our Father, the Most Hon. Mr. Elijah Muhammad said, before the Kingdom can come, there must be a falling away first. During the Night of Spiritual Darkness, the devil will cast one third of the Stars of God down to the ground. But a New Son and a New Day under the guidance of the Great Mahdi, will come. And he will turn the hearts of the children back to Our Father, the Most Honorable Mr. Elijah Muhammad.

The answer to why we (New World Nation of Islam) quote what The Honorable Elijah Muhammad wrote is simple. He teaches us, "Leave my teachings as it is." *(How To Eat To Live Book 2 pg. 75)*

Our Father also orders us all to look forward to the **Future Mahdi** in these words:

"They soon learned that Jesus was not that prophet. Muhammad, born in the Seventh Century after the death of Jesus, the last sign of that last one coming with Allah (God) in the judgment or end of the world of devil's rule. Muhammad turned on the light (Islam) in the ancient house (Arab Nation) that had burned low since the time of Ibrahim (Abraham) and cleaned it up for the reception of a much brighter light of the Mahdi (Allah in the Person) and His people, which will come from the West out of the house of the infidels." *(Mr. Muhammad Speaks, August 3, 1957, The Black Stone)*

It is absolutely a must that we understand that Master Fard Muhammad of 1930, came in search of one man and one man only: That is the Most Honorable Elijah Muhammad.

Read this. "Do you think Allah would come here to North America and live three years and near six months . . . three years and near six months . . . he stayed here three years and four months . . . four months, five months . . . and I were with Him, Brother every day and night! Now think over that. I was with Him every day and night. He was teaching me and every day and night! Now, He wasn't driving around all over the country—He was right with me all the time! *(Table Talk of the Honorable Elijah Muhammad, Chapter Four, I Love to see You Wise, December 1973 pg. 127)*

"He taught me for three years (night and day) on the histories of the two people, Black and White." *(Our Savior Has Arrived, Chapter Titled, The Blackman pg. 96)*

"So Joseph and Mary went together from that day on until the return of the old man three days later." *(Mr. Muhammad Speaks, August 10, 1957, Jesus History From The Mouth of Allah (God)*

Such divine truth confirms that The Most Honorable Elijah Muhammad is the one classified as he who was dead but is alive forevermore and given the universal keys and crown. But, read it for yourself. The 18th verse of the 1st Chapter of Revelation of St. John reads like this, "I am he that liveth, and was dead and behold I am alive forevermore." This does not refer now to the God, but refers to one of the mentally dead negroes, who had been dead to the knowledge of truth and self and God- and now has been brought to life (knowledge) and has now been given authority over mental death in these words: 'and, has the keys of hell and of death!'

The keys mean authority and wisdom of how to execute the authority. **Of hell** means the condition of the people of his, in hell, under a people who had killed them mentally. This key he says, and I quote, " . . . and of death does not mean the natural, literal death that comes to everyone, but it means that this key of authority and enlightenment would destroy the death of ignorance and the mental death of ignorance and mental death of people of God, in hell." *(Jesus Only A Prophet, by the Honorable Elijah Muhammad pgs. 15-16)*

"The Angel said to Baal and to his donkey, if this donkey had not seen me, I would have slew both of you." *(Numbers, 22:33)* "The donkey there means, 'If that little dumb Messenger's eyes had not come open to the knowledge that I am God, I would have killed all of you, because it's time. It's time that you should be killed.' It so happen that he open his eyes and he saw Me. He recognized Me.' Praise be to Allah. I am going to give him a Key. I am going to give Him Keys for all of them, that he can open their cave doors. Open them up, Elijah, here are the Keys!" *(The True History of Elijah Muhammad, The Meeting between Me and Allah (God) in Person pg. 50)*

"I said Malcolm, I said "Go up on the mountain top, anywhere you want. Yell out anything you want to against me. I said, "But Malcolm, I have The Key."

Not that I mean that I had a key to kill Malcolm, I mean this: that Malcolm and not one of the twenty-two million people of mine, here, can get out of here without a key from me." *(1965 Saviour's Day Address by The Honorable Elijah Muhammad)*

Of the transition of power from Master Fard Muhammad of 1930 to the Most Honorable Elijah Muhammad, our Father teaches us, "He took me with Him for three years, night and day. He said, 'Here it is Elijah, you can go now, and I can go.' I said, "Thank You." He said, 'You don't need me anymore.' Oh, Yes I do I need you." *(Our Saviour Has Arrived, The Knowledge of God Himself, Saviour's Day, February 26th, 1969 pg. 35)* At which point they had a tearful departure and Master Fard Muhammad of 1930 left.

It is of the most importance that we grasp the proper understanding of the above divine interaction. Abraham loved Lot and vice versa, but nevertheless they had to separate.

Master Fard Muhammad of 1930 and Our Father's love for each other was genuine and eternal, but both knew the scriptures had to be fulfilled.

For example, Our Father teaches us, "After Master Fard Muhammad had given to me the teachings and the work of preparedness of our people, it was not necessary for Him to remain here among us, so He took leave, as it is said in the Qur'an, that the people are not worthy that God remain among them, but He makes a Messenger of that people, that through that Messenger He will reach the people-through Him. The Bible verifies the same. So, He left and He gave me a hint about His return, but now there is just as much prophesy that He will not return as there is of His returning, because the Bible says He will send His angels and they will take care of the gathering of His people. I don't expect Him to return in person, not like that, because there is too much for us to look forward to that He will not, it is not really necessary. If He is going to send His own people- as they are referred to as angels-to gather the believers of my people, it's not necessary." *(The True History of Elijah Muhammad, The Meeting between Me and Allah (God) in Person pg. 43)*

Our Father stated in his 1967 Saviour's Day address, "You must look closely into the word, understand what is meant and say it."

Our beloved Leader and Teacher, Ali Mahdi Muhammad, teaches us what is meant by the above words concerning the angels that Master Fard Muhammad of 1930 would send. This refers to the **Future Master Fard Muhammad** and the Future F.O.I. (Fruit of Islam) under the guidance of Ali Mahdi Muhammad. Remember, Our Father told us that Master Fard

Muhammad of 1930 would **not** do the future work. But this related to us, the Black people here in America.

Case in point, Our Father said in a speech He made in Harlem, N.Y. in 1959 entitled, Love, *Unity and Justice.* "You have it there in the Bible that Adam was given the power to make everything. That's the white race. And they were to rule everything, subdue it or make it to bow to them. Even the fish of the sea, and that's right. The white man has even tamed the fish of the sea. He has tamed every animal that he captured. He has made that animal to bow to his power. Is that right? And his wisdom he has made the birds to bow to his wisdom. Is that right? He has made everything to submit to his authority. Go Adam and everything shall bow to you. Now, in the Holy Qur'an it says even the angels was asked to submit to Adam and they all submitted. Is that right? Submitted how? It would be absolutely sin for God to tell the angels of heaven to follow a sinful man. Now, how is this sin Muhammad? It is not that they was asked to submit and do as Adam says or his race tells them to do of evil. But what is meant there, these angels, means the great scientists of that *Us* that you read of there in Genesis.

In the Holy Qur'an . . . the Holy Qur'an reads, *We.* We created the heavens and the earth. *We* created man. We know what man's heart even suggested to him. *We* are the makers of the heavens and earth. *We*, not I, but *We*. That's the way this Holy Qur'an reads. They tell me, I don't speak Greek nor read Greek but they tell me, the Greek Bible uses the same, we.

Alright, now let us look and find this solution to our problem, right in this word, we. If we, I say understand the truth today. That, we was first, we will be the last. We went to sleep. Slept 6,000 years and allowed Adam and his race to rule us 6,000 years right? What are we going to do now; go back and pray to Adam to rule us six more thousand years? Are you going to ask Muhammad to submit to Adam when Adam's time is out? No, Muhammad is not going to do that. This is Muhammad's Day! Yes. I repeat this is Muhammad's Day! Muhammad is a name of God. Which means praiseworthy. One that is praised and praised much, that is God. Now it is God's Day. It is time for God to rule."

They have orders by Allah to do a certain job. Each one to do a certain job. "It's seven of them, Allah says that the job is not enough one, but seven of them will be ordered to do it, and think over it, these are not spooks, they are men. Last of all is that dreadful angel which places one foot on land and one on sea. That's the dreadful one that's the 7th one. The books says and Allah affirmed it, he lifted his right hand and his left hand to heaven. This is the way Muslims pray. They lift up their hands and they pray like that with both hands, he said in his words, 'Time, time as we know now will soon know no more.' He then cuts a shortage into gravity and sets the Nation on fire." *(The Theology of Time, July 9, 1972 pg. 118)*

"The Sun is going down in the West. This teaching will raise a powerful Sun and spirit of truth from this part of our planet by us, from whom God has raised." *(The Theology of Time, June 4, 1972 page 27)*

Finally, our Spiritual Father, The Most Honorable Elijah Muhammad, makes it plain that he would not be around to see the completion of His House (Nation) and that his son Solomon or the Son of Man would finish the work. Our Father stated that nevertheless he would get the materials.

Ali Mahdi Muhammad teaches us, "Our Father, The Honorable Elijah Muhammad, (Mercy of Allah be with Him), taught us that King David did not live to see the completion of His Temple (Nation) but his son, King Solomon built the House of His Father's desire.

Our Father said, 'Even though, I may not be around to complete the Temple nevertheless I will get the material for you." *(The House of Our Father's Desire, by Ali Mahdi Muhammad)*

There is more from Our Father that bears witness to the above.

"Some say, no one can do it, the other one may do it. The parable of David in the Bible states that David did not live to build a house' His son built the house however, David did get the material necessary to build the house but death overtook him before he was able to build it. Nevertheless, David showed how the house would look and his son came behind him and built the house of David's desire. If I am not able to build the house, I will try to get you the material." *(Mr. Muhammad Speaks, March 2, 1959, Time for Truth Know Thyself)*

May Allah in Muhammad bless each and every reader with the light of understanding and acceptance. Fly to Allah In Muhammad! The time of this world is at hand.

Peace ... Peace ...

Brother Mu-Min Ali Allah
National Spokesman,
New World Nation of Islam

PART I

The Future Master Fard Muhammad

Message to the Blackman

If He were the one to return at the end of the world, surely He would have had knowledge of the time of His return, the knowledge of the hour. But He left Himself out of that knowledge and placed it where it belonged, as all the other prophets had done. No prophet has been able to tell us the hour of the judgment. No one but He, the great all wise God, Allah. He is called the "Son of Man," the "Mahdi," the "Christ." The prophets, Jesus included, could only foretell those things which would serve as signs, signs that would precede such a great one's coming to judge the world. The knowledge of the hour of judgment is with the Executor only. *(Message to the Blackman pg.11)*

Flesh and blood cannot survive without that of which it is made, the earth. Jesus' prophesy of the coming of the Son of Man is very clear, if you rightly understand. First, this removes all doubt about who

The Honorable Mr. Elijah Muhammad

we should expect to execute judgment, for if man is to be judged and rewarded according to his actions, who could be justified in sitting as judge of man's doings but another man? How could a spirit be our judge when we cannot see a spirit? And ever since life was created, life has had spirit. But the Bible teaches that God will be seen on the Day of Judgment. Not only the righteous will see Him, but even His enemies shall see Him. *(Message to Blackman pg. 12)*

On that day, a Son of a Man will sit to judge men according to their works. Who is the Father of this Son, coming to judge the world? Is His Father of flesh and blood or is He a "Spirit"? Where is this Son coming from? Prophet Jesus said *"He will come from the East" (Matt 24:27)*, from the land and people of Islam, where all the former prophets came from. Jesus compared His coming as *"the lightning."* Of course lightning cannot be seen or heard at a great distance. *(Message to the Blackman pg. 12)*

The actual light (the Truth) which *"shineth even unto the West,"* is our day sun. But the Son of Man's coming is like both the lightning and our day sun. His work of the resurrection of the mentally dead so—called Negroes, and judgment between truth and falsehood, is compared with lightning on an instant. His swiftness in condemning the falsehood is like the sudden flash of lightning in a dark place. America is that dark place, where the darkness has blinded the

The Future Master Fard Muhammad

people so that they cannot find the "right way" out. The sudden "flash of lightning" enables them to see that they are off from the "right path." They walk a few steps toward the "right way" but soon have to stop and wait for another bright flash. What they actually need is the light of the Sun (God in Person), that they may clearly see their way. The lightning does more than flash a light. It is also destructive striking whom Allah pleases, or taking property as well as lives. The brightness of its flashes almost blinds the eyes. *(Message to the Blackman pg. 12)*

So it is with the coming of the Son of Man, with the truth, to cast it against falsehood that it breaks the head. Just a little hint of it makes the falsehood begin looking guilty and seeking cover from the brightness of the truth. Sometimes lightning serves as a warning of an approaching storm. So does Allah warn us by sending His Messengers with the truth, before the approaching destruction of a people to whom chastisement is justly due. They come flashing the truth in the midst of the spiritually darkened people. Those who love spiritual darkness will close their eyes to the flash of truth, like lightning, pointing out to them the "right way" thus blinding themselves from the knowledge of the approaching destruction of the storm of Allah, and are destroyed. *"As the lightning cometh out of the East, so shall the coming of the Son of Man be."*

The Honorable Mr. Elijah Muhammad

Let us reflect on this prophecy from the direction in which this Son shall come, "out of the East." If He is to come from the East, to chastise or destroy that of the West, then He must be pleased with the East. The dominant religion of the East is Islam. The holy religious teachings of all the prophets, from Adam to Muhammad, was none other than Islam (Holy Qur'an 4:16), they all were of the East and came from that direction with the light of the Truth and shone toward the old wicked darkness of the West. But the West has ever closed its eyes and thus making it necessary for the coming of the Son of Man, the Great Mahdi, God in person. *(Message to the Blackman pg. 13)*

The whole world has been and is looking for the coming of God. Several places in both the Bible and the Holy Qur'an refer to the coming of Allah (God). "The Coming of the Son of Man." Referring to God as the Son of Man should remove all doubts as to his being anything other than a man. *(Message to the Blackman pg. 14)*

The Son of man (Allah) must wait until His time, after the works of the devil. (II Thessalonians 2:8—9; Holy Qur'an 7:14—18). And another place in the Holy Qur'an describes them as the people with the blue eyes. (Holy Qur'an 20:102) *(Message to the Blackman pg. 14)*

Where was Moses and what time was that? What did the God have in mind? If no one has gone to heaven or seen the face of God, then all of these

The Future Master Fard Muhammad

prophets are liars. You must think these things over. You have a lot to learn if you understand it; otherwise, you are still in the dark as to the Truth. We are here to know whether God has visited America or whether He is yet to come. The hour can come at any day, because it is prophesied that it will come in an hour that you think not. Naturally, I had expected it to come at a certain day but the book said you won't know the day or the hour. If all of these signs of His coming are exhausted and I don't see any end to the World, that is to show me that it could take place at any time. If there is such a thing as a judgment of the World, as you and I believe, if there are signs that will be produced before that particular destruction of the old world, how many signs do you know of today that have not been fulfilled that must now be fulfilled? If you know one sign that the Bible refers to that has not as yet taken place, point it out to me. *(Message to the Blackman pg. 16)*

Who is the father if God is not His Father? God is His Father, but the Father is also a man. You have heard of old that God prepared a body, or the expected Son of Man; Jesus is a specially prepared man to do a work of redeeming the lost sheep (the so—called Negro). He had to have a body that would be part of each side (black and white), half and half. Therefore, being born or made from both people, He is able to go among both black and white without being discovered or recognized. This He has done in

The Honorable Mr. Elijah Muhammad

the person of Master W.F. Muhammad, the man who was made by His Father to go and search for the lost members of the Tribe of Shabazz. Master W.F. Muhammad is that Son of Man whom the world has been expecting to come for 2,000 years, seeking to save that which was lost. There are no historical records that there was ever a people lost from each other for 400 years other than we, the so—called Negroes. We have been so long separated from each other that we have lost the knowledge of each other. Even today the white American slave—masters are ever on the watch to keep out any Asiatic influence that might come among the so—called Negroes to teach them the truth. They are our real open enemies. This is no secret. The Son of Man is after the so—called Negroes to set them in Heaven and His enemies in hell. After His conquest of the black nation's enemies, the world will know and recognize Him (Allah) to be God alone. There is no problem today that is as hard to solve as the problem of uniting the American so—called Negroes. They are like a dead man totally without life! They have lost all love of self and kind and have gone all out in loving their enemies. They do not seem to want any God to do anything like blessing them unless that God blesses their enemies too. Fear of their enemies is the real cause. The time is now ripe that they should have no fear, only the fear of Allah, Who is in person among them to save them from their enemies.

The Future Master Fard Muhammad

By all means, they must be separated from the white race, in order that the scripture might be fulfilled. *"For I will take you from among the heathen and gather you out of all countries and will bring you into your own land."* (Ezek.36:24) *(Message to the Blackman pg.19—20)*

The so—called Negroes have no home that they can call their own. They have helped the white race to own a free country but they have nothing for themselves. This is the purpose of His coming, to give everyone that which is rightfully theirs. The Son of Man has power over all things. You cannot find a defense against Him in a war. Your weapons mean nothing. The power, of heaven and earth today will be ordered to fight on the side of the Mahdi against His enemies. He is the friend of the so called Negroes and not of the white people. His purpose is to take the so called Negroes and kill their enemies; although many of us will suffer from persecution and hunger. But, the good end is for those of you who will hold fast to Allah and His religion, Islam. They (the devils) cannot escape. Fly to Allah! Come, follow me. Although I may look insignificant to you, you will find salvation with us. The white race is excited and cannot think rightly for themselves. The so called Negroes, Muslims, in their midst, are a shelter, but little do they know it. *(Message to the Blackman pg. 20—21)*

The Honorable Mr. Elijah Muhammad

You say, "Who is this Allah, and this religion Islam?" Know my people, the Divine Supreme Being, has 99 attributes that make up His name, and Allah is the 100th. Surely His are the most beautiful names. He will make Himself known to the world that He is God and besides Him there is no God and that I am His Messenger, that Islam is a religion backed by the power of Allah (God) to free you from the hands of you merciless enemies (the slave masters) once and forever. *(Message to the Blackman pg. 22)*

The so—called Negroes fell into the hands of the slave—masters, who have robbed, spoiled, wounded and killed them. The Good Samaritan here would be the Mahdi (Allah) God in Person, as He is often referred to by the Christians as the "the second coming of Jesus, or the Son of Man to judge man." This one will befriend the poor (the so—called Negroes) and heal their wounds by pouring into their heads knowledge of self and others and free them of the yoke of slavery and kill the slave masters, as Jehovah did in the case of Pharaoh and his people to free Israel from bondage and the false religion and gods of Pharaoh. *(Message to the Blackman pg. 33)*

The Orthodox Muslims will have to bow to the choice of Allah. Allah will bring about a new Islam. As for the Principles of Belief, they remain the same. There will be no more signs to be watched for the coming of God and the setting up of a New World of

The Future Master Fard Muhammad

Islam. We are seeing this change now and entering into it. The devils oppose this change, and the Orthodox join them in opposing us because of their desire to carry on the old way of Islam. *(Message to the Blackman pg. 49—50)*

Allah will place those of His choice in authority in the making of the new world, and others must obey whomever He puts in authority or find themselves fighting against the power of whomever they hold to be on their side and in their favor. We must have a new world. We accept for a new nation completely. *(Message to the Blackman pg. 50)*

For God to fulfill His promises to deliver us from our enemies, He must go to war against the enemy and break the enemy's power of resistance to free us. War is inevitable. The so—called Negroes must come to the knowledge of Truth, that they have no future in their enemies who are the enemies of Almighty God, Allah. God must come to put an end to war and, that is to say, destroy those who love to make war and delight in making mischief. *(Message to the Blackman pg. 51)*

The white race knows and admits that it is only a matter of time when all the truth will be accepted by our people (to his deepest regret). I warn you, my people, discard your former slave—master's names and be willing and ready to accept one of Allah's Pure and Righteous Names that He alone will give our people from His Own Mouth! A good name is,

The Honorable Mr. Elijah Muhammad

indeed, better than gold. I am naught but a warner and a Messenger to you, my people, not self—sent but sent directly from Almighty God (Allah). *(Message to the Blackman pg. 55)*

In another place it reads: "And my mercy encompasses all things" (Holy Qur'an 7:156), Muhammad Ali says: "The great Apostle of the Unity of God could not conceive of a god who was not the author of all that existed. Such detraction from His power and knowledge would have given a death blow to the very loftiness and sublimity of the conception of the divine Supreme Being." But, until today, the true knowledge of the One, Divine Supreme Being, is known only to a few. We are daily coming into the knowledge of this One God. There are some people who think that God is something that cannot be seen or felt. A belief in God is the first principle of Islam. *(Message to the Blackman pg. 73)*

In the above verse Allah (God) in the last days of this present world (wicked and infidel) states that he must destroy false religions with the true religion (Islam). It (Islam) must overcome all other religions. The verse also teaches us that Allah in the judgment of the world will not recognize any religion other than Islam. *(Message to the Blackman pg. 76)*

Take to task all the learned teachers of religions, and they will admit that God is One and that He will have only one religion in the hereafter. *(Message to the Blackman pg. 76)*

The Future Master Fard Muhammad

It does not take a wise man to see the necessity of a new order or a new world, since the old one has fulfilled its purpose. Let the Christians' preachers and scientists ponder over the above prophecy of their Bible. If the time comes when Allah (God) will make all things NEW, will the Christians as we see them today be in that which Allah (God) will make NEW? When should we expect Allah (God) to make all things NEW? After the destruction of the wicked, their king and world. Just when should the end of the old world be? The exact day is known only to Allah, but many think that they know the year. But we all know that 1914 was the end of the 6,000 years that was given to the old world of the devils to rule. A religion used by the devils to convert people cannot be accepted by Allah, especially when it did not come from Him. *(Message to the Blackman pg. 83)*

One of its names is, "That Which Makes A Distinction," and another, "That Light" or "The Truth." It is the Book for the American so—called Negroes; and it is best that they throw the Bible in the waste pail since they cannot understand it. There is another Book that none has been able to see or read, its contents coming soon from Allah — the "Last Book," which takes us into the hereafter. *(Message to the Blackman pg. 91)*

They were created to rule us for 6,000 years, and then Allah (God) will destroy them from the earth

The Honorable Mr. Elijah Muhammad

and give the earth back to its original owners — the Black Nation. *(Message to the Blackman pg. 100)*

It is a perfect insult to Allah, who made the heavens and earth, and makes the earth to produce everything for our services, and even the sun, moon and stars — which serve our needs — for us to bow down and worship anything other than Allah as a God. The Great Mahdi, Allah in person, who is in our midst today, will put a stop once and forever, to the serving and worshiping of other gods beside Himself. *(Message to the Blackman pg. 106)*

Why is the black man just coming into his own? Because he desired to try getting experience (or trying everything) himself. Today you see every color in power but the black man, yet he is the originator of all. Now the Great Mahdi (God in person) with His infinite wisdom, knowledge and understanding, is going to put the original black man in his original place as he was at first, the God and ruler of the universe. *(Message to the Blackman pg. 107)*

He, also, is referred to as the Christ, the second Jesus. The Son of Man, who is wise and is all—powerful. He knows how to reproduce the universe, and the people of His choice. He will remove and destroy the present, old warring wicked world of Yakub (the Caucasian world) and set up a world of peace and righteousness, out of the present so—

The Future Master Fard Muhammad

called Negroes, who are rejected and despised by this world. *(Message to the Blackman pg. 111)*

This is the 1,000 years which it will take to restore peace and honor, after the removal of peace breakers. This time also includes the birth of a new nation from the mentally dead. However, the name FARD fits the context. *(Message to the Blackman pg. 141)*

We are reminded that this prayer is made obligatory; it is also binding upon the Believers (Muslims) in Allah (God) to obey Him. For in that 1,000 years of Millennium, the disbelievers will cease to be. And to those who live in that time it shall be binding upon them to serve and obey One God: Fard Muhammad the Great Mahdi, or Allah in Person. The Mahdi must restore the Kingdom of Islam and He must weed out from the kingdom of Islam all disbelievers. This He will do in His time. *(Message to the Blackman pg. 142)*

We are now living in the early morning of that seventh thousand years. The world of evil was given 6,000 years to reign over the righteous. Now, since their time expired in 1914, as all religious scientists agree, we are in the seven—thousandth year since the creation of Adam, or the Caucasian race. It shall be binding upon you to serve and obey the Great Mahdi (FARD MUHAMMAD) or else be cut off from the people of righteousness. *(Message to the Blackman pg. 142)*

The Honorable Mr. Elijah Muhammad

Give praises to Allah for converting the people to me and blessing us with peace and security. Allah is one God. He is independent and has no need of us, but we have great need of Him. It is He the Prophets predicted would come in the last days of the world seeking us, the Lost People, to save us and restore us to our own. *(Message to the Blackman pg. 172)*

This means that he received two books. One in a foreign language to Arabs and another in the original language. Both called Holy Qur'an. There must be something that is wrong about the Mother city which all the scholars agree is Mecca. Those are the last days, not in the days of Moses—only his work of correcting the ills of the Arabs in Mecca where he was born.

This was an example of what was to come or what will come. He, not Jesus, referred to the old truth which was given to either one, though the Holy Qur'an is without a doubt a true book, but it only takes us up to the resurrection of the dead not beyond. It does not give you a real knowledge of Allah and the Devil because it refers to the coming of Allah as the Bible refers to the coming of Allah.

The Holy Qur'an refers to the days of Allah, meaning in the years of the resurrection, and it often repeats that the people will meet with Allah in person, not in visions. He will return to them or give them a knowledge of that which they have done, good or evil.

The Future Master Fard Muhammad

He will not allow the good ones to enter into everlasting goodness without knowing of their good. It says that on that day Allah will give every man a book so that he can read his own account in the resurrection of the dead, especially the so—called American Negro.

They will receive these accounts literally because they are a people who must be separated, and these books will verify their actual worth. Of course, they have a knowledge of the chastisement of the wicked and disbelievers' rejections of the truth, and the righteous will have a knowledge of their right by being separated by Allah from evil doers and hypocrites. *(Message to the Blackman pg. 189—190)*

This is the divine problem. God, Himself, will liberate the Negro. Africa is trying to liberate herself from the same enemy. *(Message to the Blackman pg.190)*

For thirty—two years I have been trying to teach my people, the so—called American Negroes, the way of peace, and I have a record just that long in trying to live in peace with our open enemies. I have even warned my followers never to be the aggressors, as the religion of Islam teaches us that we cannot teach peace and then be the first to break peace with carnal weapons. I know who the fight belongs to. It belongs to Allah (God). *(Message to the Blackman pg. 212)*

The Honorable Mr. Elijah Muhammad

Allah wants to make Himself known in the Western Hemisphere that He is our God and has come to save us from the hands of our enemies and place us again in our own country and among our own people. He has said that He would do this job of delivering us and destroying those who have destroyed us. This is prophesied almost throughout the Bible. *(Message to the Blackman pg. 212)*

You might argue that this is impossible, but I say to you, with Almighty Allah (God) on my side this is not only possible but is in the working for our people and will manifest itself soon! *(Message to the Blackman pg. 224)*

I say to you my followers, fear not! If you are with me, Allah is with you, and the more they attack us, the more Allah is attacking and will attack them. The truth of Allah will be universally and permanently established. I have Allah on my side, while the hypocrites have the devils, and they cannot defend the followers on their side who are against Allah. I knew that the enemies and hypocrites were going to do this long ago, because Allah had told me of them and the evil, deceitful plans they would try to carry out. He will bring them to naught before your very eyes. As you see, their efforts in trying to oppose me are being counteracted by Allah with the conversion of more people everywhere. *(Message to the Blackman pg. 225)*

The Future Master Fard Muhammad

May He (Allah) give them the chastisement that He promised them in His Holy Qur'an and give those who believe in Him and His truth the joy of fearlessness, lack of grief and peace of mind and contentment. *(Message to Blackman pg. 225)*

Our foreparents desire was to see us free indeed, and not only are some of our people willing to betray those of our blood and kindred who died before us, but they are now willing to betray the fruition of freedom of our generations to come. Allah will help us to get this freedom of our generations to come. Allah will help us to get this freedom, justice and equality and some of this earth that we can call our own. *(Message to the Blackman pg. 227)*

I say to you who think that I am begging for some of these states, as I read in the papers, I am not begging for states. It is immaterial to me. If the white government of America does not want to give us anything, just let us go. We will make a way. Our God will make a way for us. *(Message to the Blackman pg. 234)*

I want to say to you again that this truth has come to you to separate you from the devil. I am taught by Almighty God, Allah, that he is going to destroy this world. You should try to get out of it, not integrate into it. *(Message to the Blackman pg. 237)*

He (Allah) has power over everything—small or great. He will let you kill a few of us that He may be justified in killing all of you for the murder of all the

The Honorable Mr. Elijah Muhammad

righteous you and your people have slain since you were created. *(Message to the Blackman pg. 259)*

He does not wait on a God like that. Many other such fools passed away in great dishonor and shame long before this chief hypocrite. No weapons (as it is written) formed against me will prosper as long as Allah is with me and I am with Allah, because the twain will never break. We always shall be together against the enemy and together for the believers. Some of the hypocrites have come to know all of these things, but they must be punished. *(Message to the Blackman pg. 262)*

The grief of the hypocrites is such that even the victim is not able to say his prayers. In the first place, God has closed the door and does not hear the prayers of the hypocrites when He sends chastisement upon them. This is in store for my hypocrites and shall befall them at any time – just as it did the hypocrites of 1935. We actually witnessed this type of chastisement that fell upon those hypocrites in 1935. One of the hypocrites then was my own brother, and another was a minister by the name of Augustus Muhammad, my top assistant at that time in the Chicago Mosque No. 2. They felt proud after they had acquired a little wisdom and thought that they were more powerful than the teacher. *(Message to the Blackman pg. 263)*

There have been many who have risen up in Islam in the past who went in the name of the Mahdi but

The Future Master Fard Muhammad

were not the true Mahdi. Even to the late Maulana Muhammad Ali, who also claimed himself to have been Christ, the Messiah, when he was among the Christians, the Jews, Hindus, and among the Muslims, their Mahdi.

Today, that has all been hushed up and passed. The world does not look to him as having been their Mahdi or the Christian's Messiah. Old Orthodox Christians, like old Orthodox Hebrews have expected a return of their once great spiritual leaders or prophets, Moses and Jesus, who taught, as the Christians teach today, a return of the Jesus at the end of the world.

Old Orthodox Muslims preach a return of Muhammad of 1,400 years ago, or that there will be no need of another prophet after him, for he settled everything. They do not take the slightest thought that these prophets could not have been the last who would usher in the Judgment. There have been so many things that have come to pass since that time that someone is needed to enlighten the people as to these latest events and to serve as a guide for the people into the presence of God.

What the Prophets brought to the people 4,000 years ago was for that people for the next 2,000 years to the birth of Jesus. And what Jesus brought (the Injil or New Testament) was to last until the end of the world – that is, the time and destruction of the wicked world ruled by satan and the setting up a new

The Honorable Mr. Elijah Muhammad

universal government under the guidance of Allah or Mahdi, sometimes called the Great Mahdi, to make a distinction from the many others who would be called by such name, as there are many Muslims who have adopted "Mahdi," like the many Italians who have adopted "Jesus" for their names.

The next verse (six) tells us that Jesus had in mind the end of the entire world and not Jerusalem. It reads like this: *"And ye shall hear of wars and rumors of wars, see that ye be not troubled, for all these things must come to pass, but the end is not yet." (Message to the Blackman pg. 287—288)*

I hope you remember what I said to you concerning the prepared destruction of Allah for this people and you who take part with them. Since they already have a head start, they believe they will deceive you in going along with them, ignoring the call of Allah and your own salvation and heaven at once while you live. *(Message to the Blackman pg. 297)*

America is the first country and people that Allah wishes to destroy, but he will not destroy them until you have heard the truth of her and of yourself. I shall continue to warn you of the divine penalty that awaits you who reject your God and my Saviour, Master Fard Muhammad. In this world of crisis and destruction of
nations, the only escape you have is in Allah and following me.

The Future Master Fard Muhammad

The non—Muslim world cannot win in a war against Allah the Great Mahdi, with outer space weapons or inner space weapons. It does not matter, for He has power over everything — the forces of nature and even our brains. He turns them to thinking and doing that which pleases Him. The great waste of money to build your defense against Him or the Third World War is useless. *(Message to the Blackman pg. 298)*

Shall you be the winner in the Third World War? The God of Justice (The Son of Man, the Great Mahdi) shall be the winner. He is on the side of the so-called Negroes, to free them from you, their killers. As it is written: *"Shall the prey be taken from the mighty or the lawful captives delivered? But thus saith the Lord even the captives of the mighty shall be taken away and the prey of the terrible shall be delivered; for I will contend with him that contendeth with thee. I will feed them that oppress thee with their own flesh; and they shall be drunken with their own blood. As with sweet wine and all flesh shall know that I, the Lord, am thy Savior and thy Redeemer."* (Isa. 49:24 —26).

We, the so-called Negroes, are the prey. Thou are the Mighty, the terrible ones, thanks to Allah, the Greatest, who is with us, to save and deliver us His people - 20 million members of the Tribe of Shabazz - who must have some of this earth, that they can call their own. Their God will give it to them. But woe

The Honorable Mr. Elijah Muhammad

unto you, the unjust judges, for the Son of Man shall destroy thee and give the kingdom to the slave. He is not to come. He is here! Believe it or not, I seek refuge in Him from your evil plannings. *(Message to the Blackman pg. 299)*

    A religious war between the two great religions of the earth and their believers, namely, Islam and Christianity; of course Buddhism will also be involved. The hereafter: there the righteous will make unlimited progress; peace, joy and happiness will have no end. War will be forgotten; disagreement will have no place in the hereafter. The present brotherhood of Islam is typical of the life in the hereafter, the difference is that the brotherhood in the hereafter will enjoy the spirit of gladness and happiness forever in the presence of Allah. The earth, the general atmosphere will produce such a change that the people will think it is a new earth. It will be the heaven of the righteous forever! No sickness, no hospitals, no insane asylums, no gambling, no cursing, or swearing will be seen or heard in that life. Fear, grief and sorrow will stop on this side as a proof. Everyone of us who accepts the religion of Islam and follows what God has revealed to me, will begin enjoying the above life here. *(Message to the Blackman pg. 303—304)*

    I never felt the like before. Islam is heaven for my people. They will see their God in truth, the righteous

The Future Master Fard Muhammad

will meet and embrace them with peace. *(Message to the Blackman pg 304)*

QUESTION: How would you describe your mission?

ANSWER: My mission is to give life to the dead. What I teach brings them out of death and into life. My mission, as the Messenger, is to bring the truth to the world before the world is destroyed. There will be no other Messenger. I am the last and after me will come God Himself. I do not say I will live so long as that, but when God comes, if it pleases Him, I may be with Him. However, if I am not with Him, this is the final. The truth I bring will give you the knowledge of yourself and of God.

I will admit the so—called Negroes educated and trained by you and your kind will never be able to maintain self—rule. But they are now reaching out for Allah and Islam, and for training from others of their OWN Nation who are and have been independent long before you were even created. We all know that you hold back the very key of knowledge that would make the so—called Negroes, that you school, from ever being capable of self—government. But they will get it in Islam. And when they have finished their courses, they won't even think of building a government on your basis. The world that you have built is nothing compared to that which Allah will build with your slaves (the so—called Negroes). *(Message to the Blackman pg. 339)*

The Honorable Mr. Elijah Muhammad

"You said that if the Africans of America had self—respect and ability they would go to Ghana and help build a great African Nation. But not with your schooling! If you would stop interfering with those who are trying to qualify themselves for a return to their Native people and country, within a few years they all would leave you and your evil doings. But nay! You don't want them to leave your country. No! Not any more than Pharaoh wanted to see his slaves leave Egypt. But Allah is going to take yours as He took Pharaoh's slaves, believe it or not. *(Message to the Blackman pg. 339)*

PART II

The Future Master Fard Muhammad
The Fall of America

Justice is a common thing. Yet, it is elusive. Men have sought its meaning and substance since time began. Plato shrugged that justice was nothing more than the wish of the strongest members of society. Jesus equated justice with brotherhood. Shakespeare saw it as a matter of mercy. I am here to tell you that justice is the eventual working out of the will of God as indicated in the fundamental principles of truth. Justice is the antithesis of wrong, the weapon God will use to bring judgment upon the world, the purpose and consummation of His coming.

Although we are the chosen of God, when it comes to justice, the so—called American Negroes are the most deprived people on the planet earth. Had justice prevailed, there would be no need for a day of judgment to come today to plead, not to the unjust judges of the world, but to the just judge to give the Black man of America justice. That just judge is Allah, God. We have come to the end of the days of the unjust judges. Even though it may offend some,

The Honorable Mr. Elijah Muhammad

you must know the truth of it all. *(Fall of America pg.2)*

How mistaken you are to assume that Jesus was the final word of truth. Jesus Himself admitted He could not tell it all. Yet He promised that God would send one who would not only reveal the ultimate truth but Who would reveal it to the people lying in the mud of ignorance and shame. We, the fools of the world, would be the first to know that truth, not the wise of this world. This is not cause for offense: for when God said He would reveal his truth to the fools of the world, it was a blessing, not an insult to us. After all, this names us His chosen people.

Thus it is that the problem of the Black man in America has set off an era of troubling throughout the world. Until your problem is solved there will not be peace for anyone. Today, then, is a new day dawning in a new world; for the old day and the old world have passed away.

The new day, the new world, if you please, cannot come into full meaning until justice comes to our people. The burden is not our oppressor's alone. Much of it is upon us. The time has come when we must speak or die. Our leaders, or so—called leaders, are choked by fear. Such a leader is not worth the salt that leavens his bread. *(Fall of America pgs. 3—4)*

Secondly, I must tell you the truth about the day of judgment. You have been taught that one day the dead in God shall rise again. You have taken that to

The Future Master Fard Muhammad

mean that people will get up from the graveyard and walk about. That is so much nonsense! Properly read, the resurrection means that we, the Black men of North America, will rise from mental death. Realize who we are! Discover who God is! Name the devil for the beast that he is! Then, like Joseph, go on to become master in the land wherein once you were a slave! *(Fall of America pg.17)*

This is the problem to be solved. If it is to be solved then how shall it be solved: and what is the best method to use in the solution? It must be a solution that touches, not only the enemy, but those who cleave to him while defying the wrath of Almighty Allah (God). It is incumbent (says the Holy Qur'an) that Allah give life to this mentally dead so—called Negro. It is also made incumbent in the Bible where Ezekiel declares (in his vision) that all of the dry bones were resurrected. *(Fall of America pg.19)*

Some of the devil's disciples are called "father" after the pope, the chief father of Satan's religion, Christianity. The pope claims in the Bible, that he will sit in the sides of the north and be like the Most High. Isa.14:13—14. And yet Allah (God) promised to pull him down to hell (Isa. 14:15). And Allah is going to pull him down real fast. *(Fall of America pg. 22)*

But since they are the devil's disciples, he should kill them if they do not obey him. That is right, if the

The Honorable Mr. Elijah Muhammad

devil wants to be a God like Allah, for Allah will kill those who do not obey him! *(Fall of America pg. 22)*

Never have we, the Black man, been so happy to be called Black. And the Book (Bible) teaches us that God will come one day and God will choose us, the Black people, to be His people. *(Fall of America pg. 26)*

Murder the Black babies? —The only ones he should be thinning out is himself. The earth belongs to the Black People. What do we look like cutting down on our birth rate. Is there any narrowing of the earth for Us? The earth is being expanded for us. There is plenty of earth for us, for Allah (God) will clear the earth of its wicked population. All of those places will be taken by the Muslims.

This is our earth. Have they squeezed it up so that there is no place to live, except they kill off the Black people? No. Black brothers and Black sisters, I hope that you will read this and understand that we, the Black people, are the true owners and Allah (God) is giving our earth back to us.

This is what he means as well as the spiritual religion of us, when He says, "Accept your own." This is our earth. He is telling you to accept it. He will give it to you.

The Bible teaches that "The meek shall inherit the earth." The humble, poor people they will get the earth, for it belongs to them. *(Fall of America pg. 30)*

The Future Master Fard Muhammad

Why should we give our babies to the enemy to be destroyed because he says you have nothing to feed them with? Follow me and I will show you: you will get more houses than you need and more money than you can spend. Help me, brothers, and Allah (God) will not deprive you of your good reward. I know you understand. What we do for Allah (God) He will do it for us. In this day and time we are all tried— the wicked and the righteous are both tried. *(Fall of America pg. 31)*

From the visit of God, in the Person of Master Fard Muhammad to Whom Praises are Due forever, the Time, now, has come to us, as it is written. That on the Day of Judgment, we will see God as He Is. (Bible: Rev. 1:7)

The Rise Of The Dead, does not, by any means, mean what you and I were taught when we were little boys and little girls; and even while we are little boys and little girls in man and woman age, we are still pushed on a baby side, for understanding of the truth.

We, the Black People, are no longer babies. We are babies to no one, except, God Himself! You are fast learning that you are not babies any more but on your Rise Up From The Dead knowledge of Black self, and others.

You are learning fast that Allah (God) Is Fast creating in us a new way of thinking, for the way in which we had been thinking was in a way of untruth

The Honorable Mr. Elijah Muhammad

and an unseemly way of understanding. *(Fall of America pg. 39)*

But this snake (white race) has overtaken us and he has bitten us so many times that we have become so poisoned from his poison getting into our blood, from his sting, that it has taken God, now, to Come to prevent the snake from continuing to sting us.

And Allah (God) has the Cure for our being bitten by the snake. He will Separate both of us from being involved with each other so the snake's poisonous sting will not affect us. *(Fall of America pg. 41)*

The coming of Allah in search for the Black lost members of their nation today is to make Himself known, so He can conquer our captors by using weapons against which they have no power. He (Allah) will bring attacks of divine judgment of their world without the use of contrived weapons. *(Fall of America pg. 52)*

We have been deceived of righteousness, justice, and equality by the arch deceiver. We have been taken from the knowledge of self as being the true people of God and that God is present seeking us to place us again in the orbit of the Divine Supreme Being where we can rotate in submission to the will of God as the entire universe is doing — except the white race. *(Fall of America pg. 53)*

This the God of justice and truth will force you to do, before He will be defeated, His purpose and aim

The Future Master Fard Muhammad

is to reunite us to our own. He will fight the arch deceiver with the forces of nature and with His own wisdom, which has no equal, to make you and the enemy bow to His will. *(Fall of America pg. 54)*

It is up to America, if she wants to help us. It would be a great good, putting us on the way to self, by any evil one or nation. The God of justice would grant them a reward for doing such, as no good act goes without its reward. *(Fall of America pg. 55)*

Christ means the "One Who is coming at the end of the world of the wicked as a crusher." His name actually means "One who is anointed to crush the wicked." The real satanic people are the white race who have disguised themselves to deceive the Black people to follow them. They just use the name, Christian, which means to be Christ—like.

They have set up a head for their religion in Rome, Italy, with the pope or father who represents himself as being the intercessor or vicegerent; meaning one who is second only to Christ or God and intercedes for the people's sins and recognition of God. But he has no Divine backing.

This false regime should be destroyed by the Christ, the Crusher of the wicked, the Great Mahdi of Islam (Allah 'God' in person).

These are the days of God's or Christ's presence to destroy this evil world with all the deceptions that the people should again labor under a wicked and merciless ruler, the devil. The presence of Allah has

The Honorable Mr. Elijah Muhammad

upset the devils who have had and exercise total control over the world under falsehood and have made evil to appear fair—seeming.

The so—called Christian world has never before displayed such madness as they do today. Since they cannot hide their real wickedness and deceitful ways, they are angry.

According to the preaching and teaching of Christianity, they prophesy that they alone would be the happy group that would welcome the coming of the Messiah, the Christ, or the Mahdi. But the Bible condemns them; that they were angry and sought to hide their faces from Him (God). *(Fall of America pg. 57)*

So the coming of the Just One makes manifest to you this evil race of sinners. And they will be against His (God's) presence; be angered because of Him and will seek to destroy Him and His messenger as it is prophesied (2nd Psalms). *(Fall of America pg. 58)*

Now the time of God has arrived — the time that Allah (God) must separate the Black slave and his white master, and bring freedom to the Black slave.

So we see the power of our enemy being broken by God in destroying the power of the white man: power to maintain his sway over the whole world. *(Fall of America pg. 75)*

I thank Allah in the Person of Master Fard Muhammad, to Whom praise is due forever, who has

The Future Master Fard Muhammad

come to deliver the Black man in America and to kill our oppressors. *(Fall of America pg. 81)*

Vote for Allah and for His servant, Elijah Muhammad and by the power of our Allah (God), who has come in the Person of Master Fard Muhammad, to Whom praise is due forever, all the prophesies of the Bible of what He will do in freeing the Black man of America will be fulfilled. *(Fall of America pg. 81)*

Here in America, Almighty Allah (God) wants to make himself known with both the punishment and the destruction of this mighty, powerful, and rich people. *(Fall of America pg. 83)*

It is time that God intervenes to bring about an end of such people as the wicked of America. She offers the same filth to all of the civilized of the earth, and she hates you if you are against her way of life and will threaten you with death as the Sodomites did Lot and his followers. But I say to you as the 4th verse of Revelations, Chapter 18 says: You that want to be a better people than this, "come out of her." *(Fall of America pg. 90)*

The 5th verse tells us that "Her sins have reached into heaven and God has remembered her iniquities and is ready to destroy her." Her destruction cometh quickly, according to the 8th verse, that plagues of death, mourning and famines which cometh in one day (one year) then after that she shall be destroyed by fire, utterly burned.

The Honorable Mr. Elijah Muhammad

This is backed up by the words: "Strong is the Lord God who judges her." Here it gives us a knowledge that He who judges is well able with power, with wisdom, and with deliberate and careful maneuvering to make judgment against her. *(Fall of America pgs. 90—91)*

Allah (God) has come to take over and to guide another people into setting up a better educational system for the people of whom He Himself is the Head. And we all get guidance from Him, as Daniel said in his prophesy, "God will set up a kingdom and He will leave it into the hands of others, but He Himself will guide it." But first He must remove all the rubbish of this white man's world educational system. He discards America's educational system, as we discard rubbish to be burned up. *(Fall of America pg. 93)*

This is the end of America. Allah (God) will destroy her for she is the most evil one of the white race. America is more evil than Europe. America is worse than her father, England. *(Fall of America pg. 97)*

Black Man, this is the end of the rule of the white man. Allah (God) came to Kill them for mistreating the Black once—slave here in America. Allah (God) says in Isaiah (Bible) that He will kill our enemy and call us by another name, Black Brother, this is going on right in your eyes, but you still think that the time is prolonged to the distant future and that you will not

The Future Master Fard Muhammad

live to see it. But, I say to you all, in truth, that you are living in it now.

The scientists of America know that America is on her way out. And since you, Black man, are the righteous perhaps all of you will be saved; for you are bound to submit when you see what is coming. Allah (God) will take you and me and call us after His own name. As I have preached to you for years, as long as we go in the name of the white man we are his people to serve him and to go to his doom with him. *(Fall of America pg. 102)*

The dissatisfied must be removed from the satisfied of Allah (God) and His people of righteousness. The lost—found Black aboriginal people in America have the greatest gift coming to them of any people who lived in the past. They will have a new growth put into them and they will be changed in the twinkling of an eye, as it is written in the Bible and in the Holy Qur'an. This change will take place after Satan has been conquered and cast out of the earth from among the aboriginal Black people to whom the white man is no kin. *(Fall of America pg. 104)*

The master must give up his slave and the slave must give up his master, regardless of his desire to remain with his master. It is the purpose of God, Himself to separate the two so that He can give the slave justice and equal chance for survival, as the

The Honorable Mr. Elijah Muhammad

slave master has been exercising power over the slave. *(Fall of America pg. 105)*

Rev. Ch. 12 (Bible) prophesies of America under the worst names that could be given to a human being: serpent, snake, Satan, devil, and the deceiver of the people of the earth. Therefore, the Black man is warned in Rev. 18:4, ". . . Come out of her, my people . . ." This scripture warns the Black man to give up Babylon, which is a symbolic name, meaning America. America has tormented the Black Man. Now a tormentor is after her. The Divine Tormentor, says that we should not be partakers of the divine torment coming against America from Allah (God) Who came in the Person of Master Fard Muhammad, to Whom praises are due forever. This means, "separation." We must separate ourselves from America so that we will be saved from the stroke of the Master Who Is God Himself. Allah (God) is whipping America with all kinds of calamities. *(Fall of America pg. 108)*

Again, I repeat, the Bible prophecy . . . "As thou has done, it shall be done unto thee." There is no friend for America. Also it is written in the Bible, "In the day of thy fall, none shall help thee . . ."

Why? Because you, America, have been and are an aide of the destruction and fall of other peoples. So who should help you in the day of your fall? This is what Allah (God) wants to bring home to America through His prophets. *(Fall of America pg. 110)*

The Future Master Fard Muhammad

We have past histories that teach us of the fall and rise of many nations. However, in this day — after this destruction of the nations, there will be no rise of these destroyed nations because Allah (God) Who came in the Person of Master Fard Muhammad to Whom praises are due forever, will destroy those who cause evil to spread far and wide. He will destroy those who love to make war on others, as it is written, Ps. 68:30. *(Fall of America pg. 120)*

A people who are that wicked against the Black slave, whom they have had for four hundred years — Allah (God) should not have any pity on His destruction of them — nor should the nations of earth pity white America, because white America is wicked beyond your and my imagination. *(Fall of America pg. 121)*

White America wants to destroy our lives. White America is planning to destroy our lives, but Allah (God) too is planning, and Allah (God) is the Best of the planners. The fall and rise of nations! *(Fall of America pg. 122)*

We have many Muslims in these lands and to try to interfere with the success of the Muslims in America, which is coming from Allah (God) Himself — Allah (God) will continue to confuse America; and she will have the loss of her victory in any land and among any people on earth. Fall and rise of nations! *(Fall of America pg. 123)*

The Honorable Mr. Elijah Muhammad

The Black people of America today are called His chosen people by God Himself, chosen by Him to build a new government based upon truth, freedom, justice and equality. This type of government is to live forever and never to be removed from the people, according to Daniel's prophecy of a kingdom of God set up in the last days — the government of which will not be left to the people. God Himself will be the head and the ruler. *(Fall of America pg. 133)*

This showed that God was going to plague Babylon; and that His people should not suffer the divine plagues sent upon Babylon. They are ordered to flee out of her. (Jeremiah 51:45.) This is a future prophecy of a future Babylon similar to the ancient Babylon under the rule of Nebuchadnezzar. The history of these two kings of ancient Babylon teaches us that they held slaves who were trying to serve the right God.

The coming of Allah in the Person of Master Fard Muhammad, to Whom praises are due forever, was for the deliverance of the lost—and—found people (Black) from a four hundred year—old enemy who has never shown them anything but evil, murder and death. Being very angry, as it was written of Him and as I know it to be the truth, He desires nothing more than freedom, justice, and equality for us, the once lost and now found Black members of our nation, the original Black nation of the earth.

The Future Master Fard Muhammad

America now is at war with God through God's people (the so—called Negro.) The confusion and the plagues of the country with disasters, one after another, is divine retaliation against white America's evil doings and intentions, against her once—slaves and her false friendship, which has her opening her homes to integrate the people of God with them who by nature are different or foreign. The white man has poisoned our people's minds so thoroughly that they fight against their own God and salvation to gain the favor of their own enemies.

The call of Islam, the true religion of God to us, the once—slaves of America, is the same call telling us to flee out of the American way of life so that our lives may be saved from the divine destruction of a non—repentant enemy (Jeremiah 51:45.) Divine plagues and foreign wars are now destroying the American standards of life and money. Her deceitful, filthy temptations, now being displayed before her once—slaves in the world, are designed to make the once—slave an enemy of his God and of his own salvation; and are designed to make them take part with them against the aim and purpose of Allah, which is to set the so—called Negro in heaven while he lives. *(Fall of America pgs. 134—135)*

The term, "a cage" — this tells us that her cities and her country became a cage for people of filth. The Bible teaches us that the God referred to the people of Sodom and Gomorrah as being people

The Honorable Mr. Elijah Muhammad

whose doing and work was such that it came up and stunk in His nostrils. (But I think that if the God would get a good smell of this modern wicked filth here He would think the smell of Babylon in His nostrils was like the smell of a flower compared to the wickedness of today.) *(Fall of America pg.139)*

Since we the Black people were kidnapped and forced into this world (of the white race) we must be forced out of this world. It is not that you my people will accept by just having the freedom to accept of your own choice. No. You will have to be punished, divinely beaten and destroyed until you accept Master Fard Muhammad, to Whom praises are Due forever, as your God and Saviour, as I and thousands of my followers are doing. *(Fall of America pg. 143)*

I warn you my Black brother and Black sister that unless you believe in Almighty God Allah, Master Fard Muhammad, as I do and receive the name of the holy and perfect God you will never see the hereafter. The Bible warns you and me that on the final destruction of the wicked, Allah (God) will say to the angel that He has to usher in the judgment to bring His people to Him everyone that is called by His name. For He gives His people His name so that He may save them. So that they may be the servant of Allah (God) as they were the servant of the white slave—master.

As long as you are in the name of the white slave—master, you belong to the white slave—

The Future Master Fard Muhammad

master. And regardless to what you believe and regardless to how mighty you think that you are, you will not be accepted by the Black people and the God of our Black people if you have the name of white people and if you are in the religion called Christianity. *(Fall of America pgs. 143—144)*

Master Fard Muhammad, Who is Allah in Person, wants to make it clear that He has chosen the American so-called Negroes to be His people. The truth that He gives to them and they, themselves, are sacred before His eyes and the world of the righteous. Showing disrespect to God and His people is inviting the punishment and doom of God. *(Fall of America pg. 145)*

The great and dreadful days of the Lord have now come to America — the land and people who worship evil and indecency. Robbery, murder, rape, famine and deceit are the order of the day in America.

If there is anything like a God of Righteousness — if there is anything like a God of Truth — should not He raise himself up and take His place and put an end to such evil as is now going on in America?

People cannot walk the streets of America today without subjecting themselves to robbery, murder or rape. America is a wicked land . . . everyone is against the other.

Righteousness, justice and freedom are despised and fought against regardless to the clear knowledge

The Honorable Mr. Elijah Muhammad

of God's hourly punishment and destruction of America by his divine plague of storms. But this is as it is written of America in the Book of Revelations, in the Bible . . . they continue their evil way and did blaspheme the God Who has power over the plagues. They hated the name of Allah, the Great Mahdi . . . they hated the name of His Messenger . . . but nevertheless that does not stop the judgment and the destruction of America. *(Fall of America pg. 147)*

The white man has had his way of ruling the Black people for so long that he thinks that he still has the power to do so while in reality the white man has come to the end of his time of power to rule the Black people.

Regardless to Allah's (God's) Retaliation to the white man for his evil acts done to the Black man, the white man still keeps inviting the retaliation of Allah (God). The white man must remember that he cannot win today over Allah (God) and His Servant, for He has power over the fraction of an atom.

The judgment of America. Judgment has come to you America. Woe to you who seek to fight against Allah (God) and against His aim and purpose. Woe to you America. Allah (God) has made you blind to His judgment and therefore you are committing suicide. He has made you blind on purpose . . . to give you the full dose of His wrath, for when a man does not know the danger of fire, then he can fall headlong into it.

The Future Master Fard Muhammad

America has mistreated the Black man for four hundred years and she does not think that there is ever a God Who will accept her Black slave and return on her head the injustice done to her Black slave.

This is the day and time in which America could benefit from what Allah (God) has revealed to me and from the work that I am doing among my Black people . . . turning them from doing evil into righteousness. As it is written in the Bible, "Babylon could have been healed;" and there was a possible chance for her healing, if she had not gone to the extreme by making fun of the God of the Jews and their temple in Jerusalem and belittling the power of the God of the Jews, to retaliate. *(Fall of America pgs. 147—148)*

The four (4) Great Judgments that Allah (God) promises to destroy America with are now coming upon her . . . hail, snow, drought, earthquake. Allah (God) has reserved His treasures of snow and ice to be used against the wicked country America in the day of battle and war. These are some of Allah's (God's) weapons, the storms that we see going on. *(Fall of America pg. 149)*

America is just beginning to experience sorrow, mourning, grief and distrust from the anger of God and man.

According to both the Holy Qur'an and the Bible, there will be plenty more of the same. In these two

The Honorable Mr. Elijah Muhammad

books, one can easily find everything foretold that is happening today. The time will grow so troublesome that (according to the Holy Qur'an) children will become gray headed, and (according to the Bible) great heart failure will become a disease upon the people, who have the anger of God (the American people). *(Fall of America pg.151)*

Woe to America, the murderer and deceiver of the people. The God of Justice and Truth has pronounced a judgment against thee — and by no means will you escape. You have made mockery of Him, God, and His people and His word, the truth. *(Fall of America pg. 152)*

The four great judgments that Almighty Allah (God) is bringing upon America are rain, hail, snow and earthquakes. We see them now covering all sides of America, as the Holy Qur'an prophesies curtailing on all her sides. And these judgments would push the people into the center of the country, and there they would realize that it is Allah (God) Who is bringing them and their country to a naught. *(Fall of America pg. 154)*

Job prophesied that Allah (God) has His weapons stored up to use in the day of battle and war with the wicked. He just takes some snow and covers them up. The Holy Qur'an says that Allah (God) destroyed people with just cold wind. He froze them. Do you think that you can get away with fighting Allah (God)? No wonder the second Psalms says that He

The Future Master Fard Muhammad

will sit in the heavens and laugh at those who are trying to fight against Him. He will have you crazy. It is true.

The heads of the governments of the Christian world are confused, and they do not know that they are confused. Why? Because their greatest desire was to confuse us. Now Allah (God) has taken the confusion out of us and put it into them. Eat, America. Help yourself to the dessert that you have prepared for us. You eat it. All praises are due to Allah (God) Who came in the Person of Master Fard Muhammad. *(Fall of America pgs. 155—156)*

Snow is prophesied to be one of the weapons that God will use against the wicked (America), Job 38:22, 23. Hail also is mentioned in the same two verses, where God plainly tells us that He has preserved it against the time of trouble, against the day of the battle and war.

The Holy Qur'an also teaches us that God used snow, rain, wind, hail, earthquakes and fire against former wicked people. *(Fall of America pg. 158)*

So this God was predicted by the prophets to come to the defense of this people (so—called Negroes) in the last days after they served the enemy for four hundred years. The Bible declares Abraham in Genesis that God would judge the people to whom his people (Abraham's) would be in bondage.

This does not mean Israel. This means the present Black people, the members of their Black nation,

The Honorable Mr. Elijah Muhammad

who have and are fulfilling their prophecy. God, in the Person of Master Fard Muhammad, will not be defeated. The more evil, deceiving, tricking and making of false promises to the American so — called Negro only increases America's divine chastisement — doom. *(Fall of America pgs. 158— 159)*

They must be separated. America will not agree to see the Negro separated from her until she has suffered divine punishment, as Pharaoh suffered. The same thing that other evil nations suffered before them is now coming upon this people. *(Fall of America pg. 159)*

Do you know why the white American does not like to talk with you about separation, and why he calls separation of the two people the wrong solution for peace between the people? He knows that it is promised and that God will do it. Then, why do they not agree with separating themselves from you and me, and we from them? Why are the Black man and white man all over the earth now in disagreement with each other to live in peace? Do you know why?

Oh, foolish American so—called Negro, seek some of this earth that you can call your own to live on in peace. Unite and ask the government for a portion of America.

This is what we need — somewhere to live to ourselves and let the white man live to himself. The two people are not brothers. They are alien to each other. God did not make them brothers to each other. *(Fall of America pg. 160)*

But a God with unlimited wisdom, knowledge and power, is now befriending the Black slave and He has chosen the Black slave to be His people. But the foolish Black people have yet to come into that knowledge; that Allah (God) is their best friend and that He is here to save them from the destruction of a people who have shown enmity and hatred to us all of our lives. America divided us one against the other. The Black man in America is so divided against each other that you seek all of the time to do evil against each other. *(Fall of America pg. 162)*

The coming of God referred to by the prophets is to unite a people who have been divided against self by their enemies. He chose these people for building a better world. *(Fall of America pg. 164)*

This is the first time since we have been lost in this part of the earth that we want to unite the Black nations of the earth into one under the guidance of God Who is now present.

Why do you (slavemasters) want to hold them; for hostages, prey? You do not need them. Your machines do the labor that the slaves used to do. Why not let them go?

You want to go to war against Allah and the freedom that Allah came to do for your slaves? Before you, Pharaoh had the same idea. He did not want Israel to go free in a land to themselves.

The Honorable Mr. Elijah Muhammad

Pharaoh lost the war against Allah and was drowned in the Red Sea. The losers of this war will land in a lake of fire, not water. *(Fall of America pg. 165)*

America's actions show us two things: Firstly, she wishes to cause fear among the so—called Negroes, with a display of many deadly weapons, but Allah is removing the fear. *(Fall of America pg. 165—166)*

You have destroyed many towns, cities and people. As thou have divided the so—called Negro, one against the other, so Allah shall divide you and your brethren. *(Fall of America pg. 167)*

Shall not the God of Peace and Justice deal with you and your troublemaking as He did with those before you?

I warn every one of you, my people — fly to Allah with me for refuge. As I warned you, the judgment of this world has arrived! Get out of their slave—making Christianity and into the right religion, Islam. The house you are in shall surely fall and never rise again. *(Fall of America pg. 169)*

The destruction and power that is bringing about the fall of the world of the white man is coming from Allah (God). In the past history of the world of the white man, there never was a time of destruction of his world like the present time. *(Fall of America pg. 170)*

One of the prophets of the Bible prophesied in regard to America, "As the morning spreads abroad

The Future Master Fard Muhammad

upon the mountains, a great and strong people set in battle array." (Joel 2:2). This is the setting of the nations for a showdown to determine who will live on earth. The survivor is to build a nation of peace to rule the people of the earth forever under the guidance of Almighty God, Allah. With the nations setting forth for a final war at this time, God pleads for His people (the inheritors of the earth; the so—called Negroes). *(Fall of America pg. 175)*

The problem between these two people — separating and dignifying the so—called Negroes so they may be accepted and respected as equals or superiors to other nations — must be solved. This is God's promise to the so—called Negro (the Lost and Found members of the original Black Nation of the earth). This promise was made through the mouths of His prophets (Bible and Qur'an): that He would separate us from our enemies, dignify and make us the masters, after this wicked race has been judged and destroyed for its own evils.

But, as I said, the solving of this problem — which means the redemption of the Negro — is hard to do since he loves his enemies. (See Bible: Deut., 18:15, 18; Psalms, Isaiah, Matthews, 25:32; and Revelations, Chapter 14.) The manifestation of Allah and judgment between the so—called Negro and the enemy of God and the Nation of Islam will make the so—called Negro see and know his enemy and

The Honorable Mr. Elijah Muhammad

himself; his people, his God and his religion. *(Fall of America pgs. 176—177)*

We want separation. We want a home on this earth we can call our own. We want to go for self and leave the enemy who has been sentenced to death by Allah (Rev. 20:10—14) from the day he was created. (See this subject in the Bible and Qur'an). No one — white, Black, brown, yellow or red — can provide to me by any scriptures of Allah (God), sent by one of the prophets of Allah (God), that we should not be separated from the white race: that we should believe and follow the religion dictated, shaped and formed by the white race's theologians.

The coming of Allah and the judgment of the wicked world is made clear by the prophetic sayings of the prophets. The so—called "reverends" and the proud intellectual class are doomed to destruction with the enemy if they remain with him instead of joining onto Allah Who loves them and who will deliver them and the Nation of Islam.

The so—called Negro masses must be warned of the grave mistake they make in following the leadership of those who love and befriend their murderers. This will not get them freedom or civil rights.

America is falling. Her doom has come and none, said the prophets, shall help her in the day of her downfall. In the Bible, God pleads with you to fly out of her (America) and seek refuge in Him (Rev.18:4).

The Future Master Fard Muhammad

It certainly will change your minds about following a doomed people — a people who hate you and your kind, and who call one who teaches the truth about them a hater. They are the producers of haters of us. We are with God and the righteous. *(Fall of America pg. 178)*

They have proved unworthy of such glorious creation, and now the God Who is the owner of this heaven and earth is ready to take over and rule it for Himself. *(Fall of America pg. 180)*

Today, God has decided that we, the Black people, cannot get along with the white man in peace, and that the white man must be removed.

The white race wanted to remove us, the Black people. But in order for the white man to remove us (the Black man) he would have to remove the whole entire heavens and make the heavens void of anything like life. Then from a void we would have to start all over again and create life, for the life in the universe is life that we, the Black people, have established.

Therefore, to get away from our own life, (which was created by the Black man) so that a new life could come in, we would have to rid the space of life, which belongs to us, the Black man — and when the space was rid of the life that we (Black people) had created, another one would have to create life of his own making.

The Honorable Mr. Elijah Muhammad

We, the poor Black people here in America, must be changed into a new and different people altogether, so Allah (God) Whom came in the Person of Master Fard Muhammad, to Whom praises are due forever, taught me.

But, not a complete make of us — we will be renewed from what we are in now — and we call it a new thing. There will come a day when we (the Black people) will have a completely new thing for man and earth and the heavens above us! But, according to the scientists, God will cause this to grow into a new thing — not a complete destruction of the old where there is no root to grow something from – not at this time!

The things that Allah (God) would like to do now, and will do, is to destroy the works of the devil — as the devil would like to destroy God's work, which God has created. *(Fall of America pgs. 181—182)*

Allah (God) wants to put the Black man back into power and the way the Black man can be put back into power is: Allah has to make the Black man all over again to master the power after giving the Black man the authority. *(Fall of America pg. 182)*

It is not hard for the Black man in America to get rich, for he is getting rich from his own wisdom. No one has given him anything.

As the Bible teaches you of the Prodigal Son — 'no one gave unto him, but he is getting rich, so fast,

The Future Master Fard Muhammad

that God chooses the Prodigal Son to become the head of the house that he strayed away from!

The future of the Black man is so beautiful that we can hardly comprehend it! The biggest thing that stands before us is qualification — and readiness. Let us get qualified to master the house that God is giving to us, before someone tries to rob us of that mastering of the house. If they rob us of the mastery of the house, I am sorry for us.

I say to you, Black brother and Black sister, do not be foolish. The kingdom of heaven will be given to you and to me. Have patience to receive it.

But, to get the house into our service, it is like a mother giving birth to a baby — the baby must mature in that which he is in. As a baby matures in the womb of the mother in order to be born, so the Black Man must mature to be born into a new world that the Black man must build himself. These are the days of trouble. *(Fall of America pg. 183)*

Who said that you were going anyplace? Heaven and hell are both a condition of life. They are not places. The devils make hell for you, and God, in the Person of Master Fard Muhammad, to Whom praises are due forever, makes heaven for you and me. *(Fall of America pg. 188)*

We are in a world that is passing out of existence — and she is putting up a fight (war) to destroy the nation of righteousness. Be aware! To try to oppose

The Honorable Mr. Elijah Muhammad

the success of Allah's truth only hastens the doom of falsehood and its teachers. *(Fall of America pg. 189)*

The lost—found members of that nation should be taught to know the ultimate aim of this world. God has visited them, and has prepared a teacher (in myself) to teach them, thereby making it easy for them to understand and recognize this world and its secret, ultimate aim. It is even given in the Bible, in Revelations 12:9. There it speaks of the members belonging to the righteous nation, and shows that through deceit, Satan causes them to become as himself — against the truth, peace, justice, safety and security one would enjoy if he only were not deceived. Under deceit, the weak minded — who have no understanding or knowledge of the arch deceiver (the devil, satan) — are made preys in the hands of the archdeceiver. This will bring about war as a showdown between the God of righteousness and the God of unrighteousness (the devil). It already has begun.

God must fulfill His promise to show Himself as God over all the powers of heaven and earth, and men on earth. As it is written (Thessalonians 2:9), "He comes after the workings of Satan." Satan has been given the power, knowledge and authority to deceive as many as he could before the appearance of God or the universal manifestation of the presence of God. He was given this power in the beginning, according to Chapter 2 and 7 of the Holy Qur'an, and

The Future Master Fard Muhammad

according to the Bible in Genesis 1:26, Revelations 6:4,8, and Revelations 12:3,4. *(Fall of America pg. 190)*

Now it is the hand of God which is after America to force her into submission – a hand from which we have no defense as it is written and prophesied in the Bible, under the name of Babylon. *(Fall of America pg. 194)*

America has enslaved all of the so—called Negroes and her evil mistreatment of them is similar to ancient Babylon's enslavement and mistreatment of the Jews, according to the scriptures. It took the hand of God to bring the king of Babylon and his people into submission to the power of God. *(Fall of America pg. 194)*

America has lived in peace — so far as foreign war is concerned. She has destroyed other peoples and their towns and cities. She has leveled them to the ground. She is still prepared to do the same with her great stockpile.

She says she has enough bombs and destructive weapons to destroy all human beings on the face of the earth three times, and still have some left. Of this she boasts. But Allah (God) has said to me that He will destroy America. He will bring her to her knees (humiliation).

The destruction sent to ancient Babylon and recorded in the Bible is the answer to most of what He has said to me will come upon the now rich

The Honorable Mr. Elijah Muhammad

America. Rain, hail, snow and earthquakes — these weapons all belong to God. America, how do you fight an army like this? *(Fall of America pg. 196)*

Jer. 50:31 prophesies: "Behold, I am against thee, O thou most proud, saith the Lord God of hosts: for thy day is come, the time that I will visit thee." Allah (God) is visiting America with great destruction which He has to pour upon wicked America.

After their mistreatment of the so—called Negro for four hundred years, she desires now to deceive them and to cause them to suffer with her and share in her doom. *(Fall of America pg. 196—197)*

All of the plagues, destructions and judgment which Allah (God) used to destroy the wicked and disobedient from the time of Adam until this day will be brought upon America. Then she will be burned with fire. This is the time of trouble that shall bring America into insanity. *(Fall of America pg. 198)*

There will not be an end to the clashes between Black and white America – and throughout the world — until wrong, evil, murdering, deceiving and robbing the poor Black man of the earth, is destroyed and righteousness and justice are practiced.

This is the day of God Almighty to set up justice and equality throughout the earth. He is to free the Black man — the American so—called Negro — from his deceitful, evil and murderous enemies.

America wishes to oppose Allah (God) in this work of bringing justice and freedom to her once

The Future Master Fard Muhammad

slaves, but this is just what Allah (God) wants. He (Allah) wants America to attack Him, to get the fight started and to bring His judgment against her with the fullness of His strength and power. *(Fall of America pg. 200)*

The false show of a glorious future that the wicked is putting on is at hand. We must remember Daniel's prophecy, that "at the end of the war desolations are determined." But before this happens Allah (God) will bless the people with a good time, as He did the people of the past, who wronged themselves and who did not pay attention to the prophet's warning among them. Allah (God) destroyed them. They thought that they were fooling Allah (God) but Allah (God) surprised them!

He made the people rejoice for a short time, with a show of great prosperity and at the height of their great prosperity suddenly, He destroyed them. This is the merciful law that Allah has put in nature.

Allah (God) lets a dying person rally before the end. America is going to do the same. America will rally and people will think that she is going to have a great future, and then the end will come in that kind of time.

America's end will not come while she is going around with her head hanging down and with heart aching and failing because of the things that are coming on her nation. No, she will be made to enjoy good times.

The Honorable Mr. Elijah Muhammad

The stock market, going up, and lots of shares being sold — this makes any man think that everything is all right. But, this is only "The Lull Before The Storm."

And the Bible warns America of what happened before her. Ancient Babylon enjoyed a fulfilling position at her time. But King Darius came against her at the time of her full enjoyment of wealth, drunkenness and her laughing at the slaves that she had made of Israel. King Darius came with his army and overcame the sleeping guards who were sleeping on the security of their life.

The Bible prophesies that the enemy will say, "Come, let us go up and destroy her whose city is not fenced in." And they will come from afar. They may come at noonday, or they may come at rising in the morning, or in the afternoon. But, nevertheless they will come at a time that you thought not.

After the war — "and unto the end of the war, desolations are determined . . . and that determined shall be poured upon the desolate." (Bible Dan. 9:26—27) I want you to know that, that which will be poured means: it is the deprivation of you, America, of your ever getting back into power again to attack the nations of the earth.

Europe will become one of the worse war areas of all the world; more dreadful than Viet Nam and other places that you are planning on going into. Asia will look like child's play when compared to what is

The Future Master Fard Muhammad

going to happen in Europe. The prophets say," (Woe to the land that is shadowed with wings." This means America whose sky is filled with planes.)

Most all of the judgments and troubles which are pointed out in the Bible are pointed at America. Study them for yourself.

America, right up to today — with all of her battles with her outside enemies, never loses sight of the inside — her poor old Black Slave — she does not want him to do anything. She wants him to be deceived. She does not want him to accept his salvation that Allah (God) is offering the Black once—slave, here in America.

Allah (God) Is Offering the Black once—slave heaven at once. This He has proven to everyone that believes in Allah (God) and follows me. I am the Door. By no means can you get by except you come by me. Your prayers will not be heard unless my name is mentioned in them. I am saying that you cannot get a prayer through to Allah (God) unless you mention me in your prayer. Try it and see. I am satisfied those who know this will bear me witness.

I have the key to your salvation, and I have the key to your hell. I can, if you will let me, pull you out of hell and set you into heaven. Then I can keep you in heaven; or I can keep pushing you and push you into the punishment of hell until you acknowledge that there is no God but Allah Whom came in the Person of Master Fard Muhammad, to Whom praises

The Honorable Mr. Elijah Muhammad

are due forever and that Elijah Muhammad is His Servant.

There is no escape for you today. The only way is through me to Allah (God). Me first, for you cannot get to Allah (God) without getting to me first.

"The Lull Before The Storm" — America is trying with all of her might to hinder you from getting into heaven. America makes promises to you, and she makes promises to me, but she does not intend to fulfill them.

Some of America's financial people promise to loan us millions of dollars; but when it comes time to do so, they vanish. But the day will come when we will be able to do the same thing to them. It is entirely up to them to make good of this day for themselves and their people by submitting to the truth themselves as the Bible says, "The Gentiles shall come to the light of thy rising."

America wants to destroy God and me, and she wants to destroy you by deceiving you against following me. America lifts up all of my hypocrites and advises you to follow them, while she knows that you will be the loser.

Look what she has done for Malcolm. America named universities after him in order for you to follow Malcolm. Malcolm turned from Allah (God) and me and started to follow them. America will lift up anyone of you that will disobey Allah (God) and myself and come to them. You see how they are

The Future Master Fard Muhammad

doing. Everyone that is a hypocrite to Allah (God) and me, America will raise him up for you to follow. America will glorify his name.

Malcolm was no lover of white people. He only tied to them in order to get a chance to fight me. But he was not a lover of them — Malcolm was a double—crosser. He tried to get to me with their help, as it is written and prophesied that he would do. His name is not written there in the name of Malcolm in the history – another name is used but his work is there in the history of the hypocrites in the life of Muhammad. He tried to take advantage while Muhammad was sick. You find this in the writings of Washington Irving and even some science writers of Islam. They can tell you Malcolm's history.

But the enemy fools you. He did not like Malcolm, but with Malcolm working against me, he used Malcolm. They knew that Malcolm had learned the history of me, and he was not able to change it.

And even if the enemy would glorify them, they will come to a naught for their time as a ruling—power over Black people, is up. They knew that better than Malcolm did. They set up for worship all hypocrites against me. Suppose we would worship China and Russia against them? But we do not worship them for Allah (God) is most sufficient — more sufficient than all their nations.

Allah (God) does not see them as a power and force against him. They are so little and weak in their

The Honorable Mr. Elijah Muhammad

power. They cannot fight against Allah (God) and win. The more you fight against Allah (God) the more you will lose yourself. *(Fall of America pgs. 203—207)*

Since the Holy Qur'an teaches that the judgment would be such that the earth itself would act as though a revelation had been revealed to it because of its perfect obedience to the Law of Allah on that Day.

Allah will use the power that is in the earth and in the sea against the world of evil. The white race think that they have control of the power of the earth, sea and air.

It was prophesied that for a time they would subdue and have the use of the power of the sea and ocean until He Comes Whose right it is to rule.

The heavens and the earth belong to Allah (God). Now it is His time to rule.

There is much prophecy concerning the terribleness of the judgment of the wicked.

The power that is in the water is in the Hand of Allah (God) to use it against whom He pleases. The earth, wind, rain, snow and ice and earthquakes are controlled by Allah (God).

It is a fearful sight to see the Display of His Power with the forces of nature bowing and submitting to His Will. I should warn you that this is now coming into action against the Western world. There will be the destruction of whole fleets at sea. Those which are capable of lying on the ocean and

The Future Master Fard Muhammad

sea bottom will be destroyed. *(Fall of America pgs. 212—213)*

Let it be remembered that Allah (God) came forth for the Redemption (to Deliver) the American Black People from their tormentors. Whether we like it or not, He Will Do This. This is the work of Allah (God) which is in effect. *(Fall of America pg. 213)*

Before the time is out, they will be forced into submission to the will of Allah

(God). This will not be done for the purpose of converting the white race Allah (God) will force them into submission to prove that He is able to make everything bow to Him in submission. *(Fall of America pg. 214)*

On the coming of Allah (God) He now makes everything bow to Him, whether you believe or disbelieve. Holy Qur'an 3:82. It does not make a difference to Him whether you are the devil or the righteous . . . all must bow in submission to the will of Allah (God), on the judgment day. We are now living in the days of judgment. *(Fall of America pg. 215)*

The 18th verse of the 11th chapter of Revelation in the Bible plainly teaches us that these nations are angry and mad because of the rise of the dead and that God Himself was the source of the power behind the Resurrection or Rise of the mentally dead people (the Black man).

The Honorable Mr. Elijah Muhammad

It is these slave—holders who have been the real cause of the mental death of the people the Revelation relates to as being deprived of Justice. God comes to give them justice and to justify them as being equal to their slavemasters as human beings. As you know from the four hundred years of legal slavery and free slavery of the American so—called Negroes, they have never been recognized even as human beings. As one devil says, they are only three—fifths of a human being. *(Fall of America pg. 216)*

This is the time of the increase of knowledge. God has given the Black man of America more light into this increase of divine knowledge than any blacks elsewhere because He chose to make for Himself a great nation out of the former slaves of America.

White America is angry at God for resurrecting the Black slaves into the knowledge of self and his slavemaster. This means that they are entering into a war with Almighty God Allah to try to oppose the truth of God preached by the Messenger of God. Read the second Psalms. *(Fall of America pg. 218)*

Allah (God) in the Person of Master Fard Muhammad, to Whom praises are due forever, has the power, and He is using His power on the wicked to bring them to their knees. Allah (God) is the greatest and there is no equal to Him. Allah (God) can take us by our own way of thinking and spin us

The Future Master Fard Muhammad

as though we are a play—toy. We cannot fight a successful fight against Him. He is too powerful. He listens in on our thinking and He is capable of making us to think and to do that which He desires to be done.

The great commotion today is witnessed by the nations of the earth, for it is America whom Allah (God) is after for her mistreatment of the poor so—called Negro (lost—found original Black members of their nation). America mistreated and killed her Black once—slaves for sport, but America's day is drawing to a close and she will not have the freedom to mistreat the Black once—slave, much longer. As the mistreatment of the Egyptians practiced against Israel came to an end, so will the mistreatment of the Black slave by white America come to an end. *(Fall of America pgs. 219—220)*

These are the days of fulfillment of prophecy of not one, but of many calamities. But in all of these preparations of the destruction of human life by the devil . . . Allah (God) too has plans to save His people.

Allah (God) has claim over the Black slave as being His people and the white slave—holder is angry because of the loss of the Black slave by virtue of this claim. Allah (God) comes to take the Black slave away from the enemy white slaveholder and join the Black slave onto his own kind again. The enemy white slaveholder hates this, but Allah (God)

The Honorable Mr. Elijah Muhammad

has the power to force the enemy white slaveholder to submit to His will.

It is the will of Allah (God) that the enemy white slave—holder let the Black slave go free. Allah (God) promises concerning the white slave—holder and the Black slave, Bible Is. 43:6, "I will say to the north, Give up; and to the south, Keep not back: bring my sons from far, and my daughters from the ends of the earth;" (America).

Since Allah (God) has now claimed the Black slave (given them the truth), Allah (God) has called the Black slave (who has accepted the truth) by His name. The Black slave who has accepted the truth of His greatness in being one of the righteous aboriginal nation of his kind belongs to Allah (God). The Book must be fulfilled wherein it prophesies that He will claim them to be His own; elect. *(Fall of America pgs. 222—223)*

Allah (God) has come and brought the Black slave the truth. If the Black slave refuses to accept the truth, he will be destroyed for willingly and knowingly rejecting the truth when the truth has come in his midst.

Calamity! Calamity in the country of America. No secret can remain hidden, for the chastisement of Allah (God) will not let you hide it.

As one writer prophesied in the Bible (Is. 18:1), "Woe to the land shadowing with wings . . ." This prophesy is referring to America which has a cloud of

The Future Master Fard Muhammad

planes shadowing the skies over America almost daily. *(Fall of America pgs. 223—224)*

The Prophetic sayings of these prophets teach us that a coming showdown between Allah (God) and the slave holders of His people (Blacks of America) must come to pass.

The time has arrived of this prophecy of a Defender coming to defend the prey (so—called Negro) who is held in bondage by the white slave holders who have and are still mistreating the prey to the extent that the world is in sympathy with the prey for justice.

Now it is prophesied that a just Ruler will come — and He has come — to set up a rule or kingdom under the law of justice for a people who have lived under the law of injustice by unjust rulers. This must be fulfilled if the next government for the people universally is going to be under such a glorious rule of Freedom, Justice, and Equality.

It is natural that the old ruler will oppose a new ruler coming to remove him and his authority to rule the people he will fight to keep his place and authority over the people. This is why Allah threatens His opponents with the final declaration of war that will end the opponents' opposition to His law of righteousness. *(Fall of America pg. 227—228)*

The time can be prolonged if the great Mahdi, the Messiah, that the world had been looking for to come

The Honorable Mr. Elijah Muhammad

for two thousand years, desires; for He does what He pleases.

This does not mean that He would change the idea of the doom and destruction of America. But if He pleased He could extend her time if she did almost a miraculous thing like submitting to the righteousness taught and delivered to the mentally dead slave (the so—called Negro). This is the only way America could exist; by bowing in submission to the will of God, taught by His Messenger.

The time that we are now in is a time of the anger of God against the evil—doers. It is a time that the God of righteous rejoices to repay the evil—doers for their doings, and to reward the righteous for their righteousness. Therefore, to curb this set day of doom, demands for the doing (righteousness) which, by nature, was not put in the white race. But they may yet be smart enough to bow to put a stay to their execution for a few days longer; not by intermixing with her slave to enjoy as long as they are blind, deaf, and dumb, and do not understand. This act only hastens their doom, while the foolish blind, deaf and dumb so—called Negro does not even know that he is being blind, deaf and dumb to his slaughter.

There is no such thing that their evil will rule peace. Also the wicked, according to the prophets Jeremiah and Isaiah, are the ones who have destroyed the peace from among men.

The Future Master Fard Muhammad

My advice to the white man is to make haste. Get in a hurry, if you want to live. Bow and submit to that great truth and righteousness, the will of Allah. *(Fall of America pgs. 229—230)*

Each, America and Russia, the two most powerful war—factors of the world, is seeking to maintain their rule over the nations of earth, and even to conquer outer—space. This will not last long. In their travel and investigation into space, Allah, (God), is permitting them to peep into His great, unequaled creation of power and might the heavens and earth. The Holy Qur'an, teaches that when Allah (God) gets ready to destroy a people He opens the doors of heaven to them. He gives them a peep into His great wisdom and secrets. But this does not mean that this adds power to the enemy to be able to war against the Creator. The reason for all of this is due to the fact that Allah (God) is setting up a kingdom of righteousness, freedom, justice and equality.

Black Brother, do not look for a high paying job drawing a big roll of money, after the war, unless with the help of Allah (God), you prepare this for yourself, which I advise you to do.

The most dreadful divine judgments that have ever been witnessed by man are now coming on America. America is the divine target because she could have bettered herself in the divine eyes of Allah (God), Who came in the Person of Master Fard Muhammad, to Whom praises are due forever. But

The Honorable Mr. Elijah Muhammad

America did not and will not better herself, as it is written and prophesied, concerning Ancient Babylon and Egypt. "We would have healed Babylon, but she is not healed: . . . " Bible, Jer. 51:9, (because she was not willing to do justice by her captive Jews from Jerusalem). *(Fall of America pgs. 231—232)*

It is impossible for America to be the victor in this universal war because of divine intervention against her. Although she has enough deadly material manufactured to try to win, can she win against Allah (God)?

She boasts of her material and being able to destroy the people of earth thirty times. If she was left free to use her material maybe America could win, but the divine die was set against her long before she ever became America.

She can try and boast of her idea of mind to deceive her Black slaves, but she will deceive herself and them. America is made manifest, by Almighty God, in the Person of Master Fard Muhammad, to Whom praises are due forever, that she is total and deadly enemy against her once slaves.

For many years, I have written that America's greatest sin is her evil done to her Black slaves. Allah (God) intends to repay her for what she has done. *(Fall of America pg. 233)*

The eyes and ears of Allah (God) are open, looking and listening to their actions. It is not necessary for Allah (God) to use mechanical devices.

The Future Master Fard Muhammad

Allah (God) is physically real and He has real physical eyes and ears. He is capable of seeing and hearing everything we do and say. He has power to defeat us in our plans which are against His plans.

The American slave—holders want to deceive the so—called Negro into believing that Allah (God) is not paying attention to them. The white man wants them to believe that he is the god that they should pay attention to.

I warn my people who believe in the idea that the white man is the god they should pay attention to. You will come up the loser.

Allah (God) is backing me up in the work He has given me to do. The work He has given me to do is for your own Black salvation. If you think that you have salvation with the white man, then go ahead with him. I am not here to force you against your own will, but I want you to know that if you are looking to white America for your salvation you are headed with them to your and their destruction.

There is no hope for America to win the war. There is no hope for the Black man in the future of America for America has no future for herself. She will not be able to win the war. *(Fall of America pg. 234)*

Holy Qur'an, Chapter 78:2 "Of the tremendous announcement."

"The Day of Decision." We are now living in the time in which we must decide on what we shall do. It

The Honorable Mr. Elijah Muhammad

is very important that we arrive at a solution, come to a definite agreement.

You, Black man of America, are holding back your decision. You are waiting because of the people who have brought this Day of Decision to us by their way of rule. Their rule is in the way of injustice.

Now the God of Justice is before us, and we must decide upon whether or not we will accept a change of rules or remain under the present rule that is passing from the scene.

We must decide rightly in order to relieve the people of the pressure of injustice. Let our decision be for the benefit of our present and our future generations.

We have no objection to that person who makes up his mind to remain in what he is already in. However, this announcement of great importance is laid before you and me so that we may come to some kind of decision: agreement on what we shall do about the truth of this announcement.

The announcement is the truth. It is asking us to decide on whether or not we are going to accept the truth or remain in falsehood. It is called "The Day of Decision." Decide this day which God you shall serve — the God of freedom, justice and equality or the same old wicked god whose rule Allah (God) is here to bring an end to. *(Fall of America pg. 243)*

We here in America do not have to wait and see; for America is folding up under divine chastisement

The Future Master Fard Muhammad

and destruction is taking place before your and my eyes. Also, the Bible and the Holy Qur'an prophesied of these days and what is going on. These days are the days of judgment of Allah (God) against the wicked.

To see 'more' may mean the end of your life and my life as it was with the people of Noah and Lot who waited to see 'more'. They could not come to a decision point of agreement. They waited and maybe you too will wait.

To wait for the truth to be fulfilled means that we will suffer the consequences of the truth — for not accepting the truth. "The Day of Decision."

As there were opponents of the prophets in the past, we have opponents of the prophet in this modern time. With all of the warning that was given before these days, we could make our decision so easily.

Remember the people of Noah had no prophets nor scripture before Noah. Again, remember that even as late as the time of Moses, the people of Moses, the Israelites, had no previous scriptures before Moses. *(Fall of America pg. 244—245)*

But again the Book (Bible) teaches that "Whosoever believe, the same shall be saved." This is truth, whether he is white or Black. If a white man, woman, boy or girl believes, even though by nature they are not the real righteous, their faith will get them out of the hell that Allah (God) threatens this

The Honorable Mr. Elijah Muhammad

world with. And their time will be prolonged. I am sure that you know this. They also know this. A remnant of them will escape if they have the faith in Allah (God) and His Religion, Islam, and Jesus prophesied in the Bible, . . . that even though an enemy give one of his least ones (believers) a drink of water, and that being an act of goodness, the God will Not deprive that act of goodness of its reward. *(Fall of America pg. 246—247)*

As it was in the day of Noah and Lot, so shall it be in the day of the coming of the son of man.

The Son of man comes to judge man and mankind. The day, the day, the day had come!

As Daniel prophesied, (Bible, Dan. 9:26, 27) " . . . and unto the end the war desolations are determined." . . . and for the overspreading of abominations he shall make it desolate, even until the consummation, and that determined shall be poured upon the desolate." *(Fall of America pg. 250)*

PART III

The Future Master Fard Muhammad

Our Saviour Has Arrived

No. 3 —— The archdeceiver. We are warned throughout the Bible and Holy Qur'an to shun this deceiver if we are members of the Black Nation (the righteous). There is nothing that is left of the truth of these people that God has not made manifest. And I am teaching you daily of this people. There are some Black Americans who will, after knowledge, sympathize with the archdeceiver (the devil) for the sake of advantage. Even some of our highly educated people will accept speaking in defense of this arch enemy of ours for the sake of trying to gain higher places with the archdeceiver. And some of them will tell me and the believers of Islam that they do not believe in any religion nor in any God of religion. The Bible foretold that this kind of talk against the truth would come in the last days; that the fool will say in his heart "there is no God."

This prophecy is now being fulfilled among even our most educated class of people. You cannot see

The Honorable Mr. Elijah Muhammad

the hereafter unless you believe in righteousness and unless you are a submissive one to the God and Author of righteousness because righteousness is the type of world that we will have to live under after the destruction of this evil and deceitful world. *(Our Saviour Has Arrived pg. 1)*

The cold and violent wind blowing for seven days and eight nights to destroy an enemy people of Allah; the earthquakes taking place, overthrowing cities and the destruction of Pharaoh and his army are to warn you and me that the same thing will take place here in America and is now going on (This is the sure truth). The evidence of this sure truth that I, Elijah Muhammad, am preaching is that America is in for every known destruction that plagued the people of old. *(Our Saviour Has Arrived pg. 6)*

As the Bible teaches us (symbolically), God says He will use every one of His arrows against the wicked world today. When a man says he will shoot all of his ammunition to try to kill you, you want to know how much ammunition he has to shoot. I say plenty; for Allah has no such thing as a limitation to what and how He can destroy since all the powers of heavens and earth are within His Hands. The forces of nature (which He is using and will continue to use) are things that we have no defense against. I say, Black Man, believe in Allah and come follow me. *(Our Saviour Has Arrived pg. 7)*

The Future Master Fard Muhammad

We cannot hope for justice from the devils when by nature there is none in them. All the day long the Negroes are mistreated. If Allah and I, His servant, will not stand up for them, who shall stand up for them? You, by far, are unable to do so; for you know not God. The devils have you afraid and worshipping that which you know not. Fear not and come follow me and God will love you and will set you in heaven at once while you live. *(Our Saviour Has Arrived pg. 9)*

I am for the separation of my people from their enemies; that they share not in their enemies' destruction, even though I may lose my own life in this daring attempt to save them by the plain, simple Truth of God and Power. It must and will be done regardless of whom or what. It can be done in one day, but Allah desires to make Himself known in the West, as it is written of Him. *(Our Saviour Has Arrived pg. 19)*

That truth comes to us at the end of the Caucasian world. The end has come and Allah has also come to make manifest this hidden truth to us, the Black nation of the earth; and first, to the lost members of that nation. According to the Bible and Holy Qur'an Sharrief, it is the divine purpose of Allah to make known this hidden truth that shall make the Black nation free. *(Our Saviour Has Arrived pg. 20)*

This is the time. There never will be any peace among the nations of earth until the so—called

The Honorable Mr. Elijah Muhammad

Negroes have heard the truth and those who accept it are separated and placed in the paradise of their God, Allah.

The so—called American Negroes, with their God, Allah, shall become the universal rulers, believe it or not. They can do it now if they will quit this slavery religion called Christianity. No Black people who accept Christianity will ever be free. *(Our Saviour Has Arrived pg. 21)*

My people, the so—called Negroes, will soon learn and recognize the Truth, for the Author of Truth is with us. They yell their lungs out over a dead Prophet (Jesus of two thousand years ago) who cannot and did not come to do anything for us but prophesize of us going into slavery and of God delivering us; and He was not even sent to us. The white race and their tampering with the Truth of the Bible (their slave making Christianity) have poisoned the very hearts of our people against themselves and their Own God. No one can unite the so—called Negroes in America without the help of Allah (God). We must think of self unity, and not love and unity with our enemies whom Allah (God) will destroy from the face of the earth in the very near future.

My beloved Brothers and Sisters who are thinking yourselves Christian, you are not Christians! You can't be a Christian unless you are white. That is the only race on Earth that is Christian; white people. I say, today Christianity is in an awfully terrible

The Future Master Fard Muhammad

condition. The Father, the god, sitting in Rome, is in a terrible condition trying to keep his people together. Look at how they are now, demanding to give them something new. Don't you see their Bible being fulfilled? And look at the name that the Bible gives to that man – a Dragon. The Pope of Rome is spoken of in the Bible as a Dragon. Think it over. And the people that he serves, as Beasts! Don't go out of here angry with me because I say what you wrote yourself.

This is what the white theologians and scientists of the Book, or their religion wrote themselves. I got hold of a little book once on the argument between the Pope and Martin Luther over some of his symbolic work that he was doing in the Bible. And they began to question what this meant and what that meant. You would be surprised. I don't have time to go through in detail. But God has given me the knowledge of the Book. And therefore I wish to tell you that you are so wrong in calling yourselves Christians. You are so wrong! There are no Christians but the white man. I'll tell you the true meaning of Christian which refers to us, the Muslims. "Christian" means to be crystallized into one. Christians are not yet crystallized into one. They say, "We are followers of Christ; that is why we call ourselves Christians." Where are your works if you are following Christ? And who is Christ? They say, "Jesus Christ." What Jesus Christ? Jesus wasn't even

The Honorable Mr. Elijah Muhammad

a Christ back then, 2,000 years ago. According to the meaning of 'Christ' that name means One coming in the Last Day or Crusher — He Crushes the wicked; Christ, the Crusher. Jesus didn't do that. That is the Mahdi who will do that today; the One whom we are representing to you; The Great Mahdi; the Restorer of the Kingdom of Peace on the Earth. *(Our Saviour Has Arrived pg. 49)*

You should remember that the time of wisdom, now, is coming for you. And creative thoughts, now, are coming to you. And the God Who has chosen you to be His People will teach you and lead you how to fashion them into actual beings as the white man has done. Our creative thoughts were taken from us until he (the white man) rules his world under his own creative thoughts.

But he had to use the same material that Our Father put here. He (the white man) wasn't able to create his materials because everything was already in the Earth. Therefore, when he was made, he had to use what we, Our Fathers, had made to fashion him a kingdom of the material that was already created. And now, when it comes to worshiping the Gods, I say; A Jesus, A Christ, A God, that is Born for you and me today! Who is He? He is what they call, "The Son of Man." Who is the Son of Man? And why do they call Him that? Because He Himself is coming to judge the Original Man and the mankind. The mankind is the white race. The Original Man is not a

The Future Master Fard Muhammad

mankind. Don't get yourself mixed up in that kind of representing — all mankind. You are not a 'kind' of a man; You are the Man! This is what I have been teaching you here. You will try to take me to task, but you can't because you don't know what material to use. As I say, I am teaching you of the God, not of the prophets. I am the Last of them.

We want and we must have, some of Our Good Father's Earth – a place for ourselves to live on; we must have it. We cannot live under or in this other shadow; We cannot do that! It is time that we live ourselves, under and in the shadow of our Own. All of this big old Earth here. Think over how big it is. It's a great big old Earth. They are trying to practice birth—control over you. What do you look like accepting birth—control? When has the Earth got too small for you? There is actually plenty of Earth for us. There has never been an exhaustion of the Earth or of the food that it burns out; it goes back down and fertilizes the Earth without aid. But everybody wants to live in Chicago; naturally someone will get hungry here. There is not enough food in Chicago to feed everybody. But that is no reason to start killing babies; just to live in Chicago. That is wrong; the Holy Qur'an teaches us. Birth—control is not even thought of in Islam. If this is our Earth, and it is, we haven't over—populated it. We still have plenty. You say "China." Well, China is a little grafted race of people, and they are piled up there in that country.

The Honorable Mr. Elijah Muhammad

They can't spread out so much because they have a boundary to the race — the Red, Yellow, and the White races. There is a boundary set for them. And this boundary, now, has been jumped by them. This is causing trouble. This is why the Original Owner decided He would take over His Part. When He takes over His Part, there will be no part left for any other part! *(Our Saviour Has Arrived pg. 51—52)*

"Fard" is a Name meaning an independent One and One Who is not on the level with the average Gods (Allahs). It is a Name independent to itself which actually means One whom we must obey, or else He destroys us. This honorable, Majestic, Person comes in the last day. The reason why we call Him the Supreme Being is because He is Supreme over all beings and or is wiser than all. The Holy Qur'an teaches: He is wiser than them, meaning all the Gods before and all who are now present. *(Our Saviour Has Arrived pg. 57)*

The Nations of the Earth expect the coming of a God Who will overcome and destroy all idol gods and set Himself up as the Supreme God over all; for all nations have made their own gods according to the Bible (Kings 17:19). *(Our Saviour Has Arrived pg. 64)*

Let us quote another prophesy of Jesus on the coming of the Son of Man; "But first must He suffer many things, and be rejected of this generation" (Luke 17:25). The words, "this generation" is not to

The Future Master Fard Muhammad

be taken to mean the generation in the days of Jesus and His rejecter's, the Jews, two thousand years ago. It means the people and generation of the Son of Man who would reject Him in His day of coming to reclaim His lost—found people; and at the same time, suffer persecution of Self and His teachings as Jesus was by the same enemies in His time. *(Our Saviour Has Arrived pg. 71)*

They never wanted Islam as their religion because they cannot live the life of the righteous. And they do not want the so—called Negroes to believe in it nor pray to Allah. Why? Because Allah will answer prayer, and believing in Him and His religion will not only get us universal friendship, but will give divine aid and help against our enemies.

We need a God who will help us and answer our prayers when we call on Him; not an unknown mystery God, not a dead crucified Jesus of two thousand years ago. But we must remember that to get something worthwhile, we must be willing to sacrifice all that we have. *(Our Saviour Has Arrived pg. 73)*

The Days of Allah (God). These are the Days of The Son of Man and the days of the removal of the old world of evil, filth, and unrighteousness. These are the Days of setting up a clean world under the guidance of the Original People (Black Nation) who were never guilty of doing evil until one of the gods by the name of Yakub discovered the essence of the

The Honorable Mr. Elijah Muhammad

Black Man to make a white man and Yakub did just that —— he made the white man.

Now since he has discovered this essence, today we are under the God (Allah) to do away with that very essence in us so that no other man can make another people who are different from us. This will never happen again. That is why you are taught that you will be born again physically. This rebirth is in order to get rid of that wicked material in the very essence of the sperm of the Black Man. This wicked material will not be in the Black Man for any one to use after the removal of the present world and people.

You will be caused to grow into a new person and the nature will be different. It will be the nature of righteousness and then we cannot sin. In that kind of rebirth it will be impossible for us to sin.

So the days of Allah (God) mean the setting up of a new world and a new people. Allah (God) Will Not even accept the names that we used in the old world.

The Holy Qur'an teaches the scholars like this that I am about to write —— I say the scholars for the average reader cannot understand it —— that after the removal of this world – after twenty (20) years you will not be able to follow and do that which you are now following and doing in this world today. Within twenty (20) years the thought of this world will vanish from your mind. You will not even be able to remember what this world looked like or what

The Future Master Fard Muhammad

went on in it. Your mind will be clean. Ask the wise scholars and scientists. They will agree with me.

Do not look for a spirit, a spook, or a formless thing. The formless is what we think in our brain. It is formless until we make a form for it. We cannot use a God or follow a God that is not something like ourselves; for if He Is Not something like ourselves He Cannot Have an Interest in our affairs.

Therefore the Bible prophesies and the Holy Qur'an also teaches us that a Son of a Man will Come to us to be the Judge of the Judgment Day. This Son of Man Will Sit As Judge. Why He Is Called the Son of Man will have to be taught to you. Here I do not have the time and the space to teach you why He Is called the Son of Man.

The days of Allah (God) means 'years' of Allah (God) and not a twenty—four (24) hour day. It means years. These 'Days' or 'years' of judgment, according to the Bible and the Holy Qur'an, will not run over twenty (20) years. And according to the scientists of Islam the teachings of the Holy Qur'an, which are to be understood, the Judgment is to take place between 1380 and 1400 years after the death of Muhammad, the son of Abdullah.

And according to the scholars and scientists of Christianity, they have it just about right too. The time that they say the Judgment will come is based on two thousand (2,000) years after the death of Jesus. This is right. And in the Bible, the Books of

The Honorable Mr. Elijah Muhammad

Daniel and Revelation, the time is given, if understood.

So we use a very quick and simple word that covers all that I have said concerning the Judgment and the Judgment Day or time of the Judgment that we are living in. And these are the days of Allah (God), the God Who Will make a new heaven and a new earth after the removal of this world, god, and people (wicked).

I am mighty sure that from what I have said here you will see the very necessity of the God changing our way of thinking and then He will change our name and give us a Name, for we never had a name of our own. All of the names that we have been going in are the names of our slavemaster (white race). *(Our Saviour Has Arrived pgs. 81—83)*

Remember these words, (Bible, Is. 65:15) . . . "The Lord God shall slay thee (the enemies) and call you (who submit to His Will) by another Name." Glory not in the name of satan, but Glory in the Name of the Lord God of Truth Whose Name abideth forever, and His Names have the Most Beautiful Meaning. *(Our Saviour Has Arrived pg. 91)*

Scientists have learned by study that everything we see that we call Universe is not endurable. It is gradually decaying. The Bible and the Holy Qur'an both verify this decay of the Universe and that one day a Wiser God than Them all will exist in a new Universe. A new universe means that it will not be

The Future Master Fard Muhammad

exactly like this one that we know. According to the hints of the Holy Qur'an, it will be a better one than we have. Naturally, after experimenting with a thing that has been made, we can improve on a new make of it. *(Our Saviour Has Arrived pg. 97)*

The Present God's (Master Fard Muhammad's) Wisdom is infinite. No Scientist can see an end to This Man's Wisdom coming in the future. That is why the Bible and the Holy Qur'an refer to Him as The Greatest and Wisest of Them All and say that He will set up a Kingdom (Civilization) that will live forever. *(Our Saviour Has Arrived pg. 99)*

His Name of Praise and of "worthy of Praise" are just a few of the Great Names Which Belong to God, and He Wants to Give Them to us. The Bible teaches us that He Will Give His Names to those who believe in Him. According to the Bible, Rev. 7:3, the Judgment cannot take place until those Who Believe in Him are Given His Name (sealed in their forehead). *(Our Saviour Has Arrived pg. 102)*

The white race was given a limited time (6,000 years) to be the overlord (white) of our earth and ourselves. He is well aware of it (time). The white man is well aware that he does not own the earth and that he had no part in its creation. The scientists of the white race well know this, but, nevertheless, as it is written (Bible) Jer. 49:21, we see that today trouble is brewing everywhere; even between Black and Black where it should not be. But where Black wants

The Honorable Mr. Elijah Muhammad

to live with white and does not want to take his responsibility to go for self, Black has trouble with Black due to this desire. Integration is against the Desire and Will of God Who Wants and must Do that which is written He Will Come and Do: Restore the earth to its rightful owner (Black Man).

The Black Nation is under the Guidance and Guardianship of our God, the Great Mahdi, He is The Restorer, The Defender of The Black Nation. He Will Restore and Defend us.

There is nothing that the white race can think of in this day and time that is not already known by the God of the Black Nation. Therefore, the showdown will be victorious on the side of the God Who Knows what we think and plan. He has power over us and over the atoms of the atmosphere. The attacker would have no power whatsoever to defend himself in a showdown against such a Wise and Powerful God. The Great Mahdi. *(Our Saviour Has Arrived pg. 104)*

The Great Mahdi has and exercises power over everything of the creation carries or brings forth power. One would be silly and greatly the loser to attack such a God. But nevertheless the world must see a showdown between the two Gods. His Eyes and Ears are ever Open in both camps . . . the wicked and the righteous. So these two worlds draw nearer and nearer together for a showdown.

The American Black Man is to be warned and he is warned of this showdown which is coming

The Future Master Fard Muhammad

between the two worlds. He should fly to God (Allah) of his people Who Has Power to save them.

My work, to bring you into the knowledge of Allah (God) and the God of your fathers and the knowledge of the power of that God and to ask you to accept your own, has been given to me. The Black God is well able to give you your own.

Fly to Him, I say. Fly to me and I will guide you to Him as you do not know Him. If you do not know, seek to know. I will teach you to know. To reject your share in the earth and the universe which is rightfully your own would be such a foolish act that it could never be blotted out of your future history.

Come Follow Me, I say. I will lead you to your God of Salvation. If you stay where you are, you will suffer the consequences. Just as a reminder, read the Bible Jer. 50:46 and II Pet. 3:10. It is terrible, awful, and frightful, to look up and instead of seeing a blue sky, see a sky of flames and fire. This will surely come. Allah (God) has affirmed this prophecy with me. The whole heavens will be blotted out and in its place there will be a canopy of flame. The heavens and elements that make up the atmosphere of the earth will melt with fervent heat. There will be an explosion of the total atmosphere of the earth by God Himself. Take Heed of it, for the Holy Qur'an says such a time as we are entering into now is a grievous time. It will make children's hair turn gray. If the grief and excitement will make children turn gray

The Honorable Mr. Elijah Muhammad

because of the terribleness of judgment, what do you think our hair will be doing? The Bible prophesies gray and baldness upon all heads. *(Our Saviour Has Arrived pg. 105)*

He, Master Fard Muhammad, God in Person, will create a new heaven and a new earth, a new Islam and new government and people. The new earth referred to is a new people who will change the old into such a great future that actually the earth will look like a new earth and a new earth will be made here in what we call America.

This is the way of the Gods. One God is not allowed to pattern after another God when it comes to universal change. He is to use His own Wisdom. The white man brought about a universal change and so will Master Fard Muhammad, Allah, (God) in Person, bring about a new universal civilization even as Yakub, the father of the white race, brought about a new universe of wicked people and a wicked rule over righteousness. *(Our Saviour Has Arrived pg. 110)*

Only the principles of the present Islam will remain the same. It is the Black man of America who is referred to as the lost member or lost sheep of his people. The awakening or rising of the Black man in America must come first because he is the choice of Allah (God) in the Person of Master Fard Muhammad for building a new heaven on earth.

The Future Master Fard Muhammad

As God created the present heaven and earth out of nothing, so will God, in the Person of Master Fard Muhammad, build a new heaven on earth from nothing (a people who are nothing) so that this world will have no claim on the making of the new people of the new heaven on earth. *(Our Saviour Has Arrived pg. 111)*

The Black man must be awakened to the knowledge of self – that he is not what the white race has taught him to be. He must come out of this hopeless state. He thinks he is worthless. He should be brought into a state of worthiness and the knowledge and reality of his great place into which Allah, (God) in the Person of Master Fard Muhammad, will put him. He is to place him on top and not the bottom — because the bottom is where he is today — and make him no more the tail, but the head. He is to become the head of civilization of the new world or new heaven or earth. He is not to rule over this people, but he is to be the ruler of self, after the rule of the Caucasian, wicked world.

You will have to look to your own God, Master Fard Muhammad, and your religion, which is peace, Islam. Islam significantly means the makings of peace, but not making peace with the enemy of peace. The so—called Negro is arising to the knowledge today that I am teaching — knowledge Allah (God) revealed to me throughout the Black man's world. *(Our Saviour Has Arrived pg. 112)*

The Honorable Mr. Elijah Muhammad

As the God of Truth, Justice, and Righteousness, Allah Is Going to Be the Ruler or the Creator of the New Government. Then by no means can He Carry any of the old world into His New Kingdom of Truth, Justice, Equality, and Peace. We must have a new government and a new people to operate the new government (Bible Ez. 18:31). *(Our Saviour Has Arrived pg. 113)*

The prophet (Ez. 47:12, Bible) says that Allah (God) will even make new trees and shall bring forth new fruit. Jn. 13:34 prophesies that a new commandment shall be given to us which will make you able ministers of a new testament 2 Cor. 3:6. And 2 Cor. 5:17 says that "if any man be in Christ, he is a new creature." Eph. 2:15, prophesies "of twain, one new man, so making peace."

The Bible, 2 Pet. 3:13, prophesies, "We look for new heaven and a new earth" and Rev. 21:5, "He said," 'behold, I make all things new.'"

Since the Bible here has promised through the mouth of the prophets, that Allah (God) Raised Up in Israel will be brought about when the God of the Resurrection of the Dead Appears, the Dead will no more be as they once were. They will become new creatures.

The Holy Qur'an teaches us that "He caused things to grow into a new growth." Here we have something which the Holy Qur'an says "is worth praying for." Under the God of Freedom and

The Future Master Fard Muhammad

Righteousness, we will grow into a new growth instead of growing into decay any more.

Also in the Bible Isaiah mentioned the long life of the righteous in these worlds: "that a person one hundred (100) years old will be like a child" . . . meaning that their age will never cause them to look old. They will have the freshness of youth says the prophet, Isaiah. And the Holy Qur'an, also verifies the same. Allah (God) in the Person of Master Fard Muhammad, to Whom Praises are Due forever — out of His Own Mouth — Said to me that He Causes us to Grow into a New Growth. And that we would have the look and the energy of one who is sixteen (16) years of age and our youth and energy of a sixteen year—old would last forever. *(Our Saviour Has Arrived pg. 114)*

Then the Bible and the Holy Qur'an verify these prophecies that everything will pass away or that there will be a gradual decay except Allah (God) Himself. Holy Qur'an Chap. 26:3 . . . "everything has a beginning and everything has an ending except Allah (God) Himself." Allah (God) Cannot Be Destroyed, for He Is the Maker of the Present heaven and earth and before these are destroyed He Brings In a New heavens and a new earth or He Reproduces the present one as the Holy Qur'an teaches us. *(Our Saviour Has Arrived pg. 115)*

Yakub, the father of the white race, did not make the white race from nothing. Yakub made the white

The Honorable Mr. Elijah Muhammad

race from us (Black Man). So he took living material (Black Man) to bring out a new people. And so Will Allah, the God of Righteousness. Allah (God) Will Take living material, the so—called Negro, and make a new people out of them. The So—called Negro, the Black Man, up from slavery of four hundred (400) years, here in America, is the people out of whom Allah (God) Wants to build a new heaven and a new earth or we say, a new people and a new government. *(Our Saviour Has Arrived pg. 116)*

We need a new everything. He (Allah) makes all things new.

Are you surprised that Allah, the God of Righteousness, Will Bring in a new world after the removal of the rule of the God of evil? The term of office of the God of evil is up. Are you surprised that you will have to accept a change? Do you love the white man's type of civilization and its doing . . . that way of deceiving and murdering? Do you love this evil civilization more than you would love a government of peace where the Freedom of Man is given and where equality is not withheld from those who are qualified to be their equal? *(Our Saviour Has Arrived pg. 118)*

What can Allah (God) do with this world of the white race since it has not come into his line of Guidance and government of people? There is no place for the evil practices of their evil kind in Allah's (God's) World or Kingdom of Righteousness.

The Future Master Fard Muhammad

To make all things new means to go to the very root of everything that exists. We are taught that we ourselves will become a new people. The Holy Qur'an teaches that He would Cause the righteous to grow into a new growth. The Bible prophesies that you (the righteous) "will be changed in the twinkling of an eye." The disciples of Paul did not know exactly what you would look like in that changed form but they concluded "you will be like Him (Allah)."

He makes all things new. Allah (GOD) Who Came in the Person of Master Fard Muhammad, to Whom Praises are Due forever, taught me that every twenty—five thousand (25,000) years, each God Coming After the Other God made a new civilization. His Belief, Teaching, and Theology were Different From the Other God Who Preceded Him Who Made a beautiful change in the History of the wisdom of man. *(Our Saviour Has Arrived pg. 119)*

In the angels' decision over the making of the white race, they said to the Maker of the white race, "What will you make but something that will cause bloodshed . . . a mischief- maker in the land who will cause bloodshed." But the Maker, Yakub, did not deny that he was making such a man; but he said he "knew what the angels did not know." He did not know what the angels did not know. The angels knew that he was about to make a man who was going to destroy the peace of the Original Man and they told

The Honorable Mr. Elijah Muhammad

Yakub, the Father of the white race, what he had in mind to do in the making of a new man from us. So does Master Fard Muhammad, to Whom Praises are due forever, Know what He is About to Do in Making a new civilization. *(Our Saviour Has Arrived pg. 120)*

The white race are the gods of their world. The white man puts us on wheels. You say, "Oh, but we had wheels before." That is all right if we did have wheels. He himself put you on a new wheel, one different from the one you were using for transportation. The white man moved you off the camel's back and the donkey's back and he put you onto fast—powered transportation such as automobiles and he put you on wings in the sky. All of this was new compared to what we had. So we would like to show you that the white man himself has made a new world. Therefore should we be surprised when the God of Righteousness Comes in and Makes a New World and that He does not want any material of the old evil world? Are you surprised or is it due to your desire to remain with the old wicked world? The Next World is a World of Righteousness. You do not want to be righteous. You want to have Freedom, Justice and, Equality. But you still would like the wicked to continue to rule because of your desire to be wicked.

The Future Master Fard Muhammad

The God of Righteousness Who Will Rule in the Hereafter Will Have an unlimited Rule and not a limited rule like the rule of Yakub.

How Must the God of Righteousness Begin? What thought do you have of Him and His Beginning? He Makes All things new. The first way to bring about something new is to change the way of thinking of the people. When you have removed from the people the old mind and idea then you can insert new ideas into their minds. This is done by the old being attracted by a new way of teaching . . . a new school of learning to condition their minds to that thing that you are about to present to them that is altogether new and different from what they have been accustomed to. *(Our Saviour Has Arrived pgs. 121-122)*

The Wisdom, Idea, and Way of Thinking of Master Fard Muhammad, to Whom Praises are due forever, is Superior to any way of believing today. There is no one to hinder His Image or Thought for that which has not yet been conceived in our brain.

He goes after the root of all things like our Black Father did in the beginning when He Built the universe out of nothing. He Is as One Sitting out in space with no material of space to Make something altogether new. He Goes after the Root in Making this New World of people.

As He said, "first He Makes a New Mind for us and a New Way of thinking." He teaches us a

The Honorable Mr. Elijah Muhammad

different education, one that we have never had before. He Gives us Education on the Wisdom, Knowledge, and Understanding of Gods . . . not of prophets . . . but of the Gods of the Prophets of the past. He builds our minds according to the way Gods Think and not the way of thinking of servants (prophets). The prophets of the past were inspired and their inspiration was true. *(Our Saviour Has Arrived pg. 123)*

I think that you are thinking that I am going too far now . . . However no education of this world of the white race will be accepted into the new world. For the new world you have a new education and government. The God of the New World is a New God. He is not the God Who Ruled from the Beginning but He Has the Same Idea of that rule as the God In the Beginning Had to create Something new.

As you notice, the effect of thoughts or your thinking at times has such deep effect on the brain that it affects the surface of your face, skin, and body. Your eyes are also affected by that tremendous thought or way of thinking that you have as it acts upon your brain.

Allah (God) makes it very easy in the next life . . . that new life. You will be happy all the days that you are in it. The Holy Qur'an teaches us that "He causes the righteous to grow into a new growth." The basis or pillar of that new world is when the old mind

The Future Master Fard Muhammad

has been changed to a new mind or our thoughts are changed to a new mind or our thoughts are changed to a new thought or new way of thinking which brings about a change of the whole body. *(Our Saviour Has Arrived pg. 124)*

He makes all things new. Go back to the very earth, as the prophecy concerning this change goes like this. The prophets say that they "saw a new heaven and a new earth." We and the earth both will be new because the Powerful God or the Supreme Being over all Has Superior Wisdom and He Will Cause everything to grow into a new world from that of the old world.

The curse of Yakub and his people veils all of the earth and the atmosphere of the earth. After the removal of the curse of Yakub there will be a new way of thinking by a new God. He is Superior to all other gods who Existed before Him. The power of heaven and earth will submit to His Power and a change is made easy and inevitable; for the heavens and the earth are controlled by the God of the Black Man, Allah, Who Came in the Person of Master Fard Muhammad, to Whom Praises are due forever. *(Our Saviour Has Arrived pg. 125)*

Here we have a prophecy that Allah (God) Will Make All Things new. "He causes things to grow into a new growth," according to the Holy Qur'an. He Would Not Be a God Who Has Power over all things if He could not Change things according to His Will.

The Honorable Mr. Elijah Muhammad

If He Could Not Make New People of an old dead people, then He Has Not the Power to Bring In New Things because reproduction is less trouble to do and does not require such a skill as it does to Make something outright new.

Here it refers to both the spiritual and the physical side, but did not He Make us in the Beginning out of nothing?

Look at our creation from sperm to that of a human being. This is a marvelous piece of work of nature which bears witness of the First Creation. We are making new creatures every day. What helps to bring about new creation? When you make a new way of thinking in a person, he is bound to do something new; for he cannot do something other than new since he has a new mind, new ideas. A new mind and new ideas produce a new thing. Just because we have not seen the creation of these things we are quick to disbelieve that they can ever happen.

The Bible, 2 Cor. 5:17 says "Therefore if any man be in Christ, he is a new creature; old things are passed away: behold, all things are become new."

"All who are in Christ is a new creature." This Christ Who is referred to in the above verse is Allah (God) in Person (The Mahdi). This is true and the scripture's prophecy teaches you that You have to be new to be one of His Followers. He changes you in mind; and as it is written "as man think, so is he" (Pr. 23:7).

The Future Master Fard Muhammad

Christ . . . the true interpretation of the Name is "The Crusher." When understood, It makes the God Coming in the Last Day to Crush the wicked to be the True Answer to that Name of Christ. You call Him the Anointed One . . . That is true. He is Anointed to Crush the wicked. He does Not Come loving the wicked as you would like Him to do since you are wicked yourself. *(Our Saviour Has Arrived pgs. 128—129)*

Behold He Makes All Things New. Allah (God) Will tear down the false one (white race). How can Allah (God) Build something new and better for us than that which we are living in if He does not first tear the false one down and Build a New house; for the old house has become so disagreeable to live in peace. We have got to find a better house than this one in which mischief and bloodshed is going on daily. Now we need another house better than this one. Read the Last Book in your Bible, Rev. 2:17, You must have everything new. Read Romans 7:6. These are references of your Bible that you believe in; now you see it verifies the teachings of Islam. Maybe now you will not accept these Bible verifications. *(Our Saviour Has Arrived pg. 130)*

God referred to this internal and external cleansing in these words (Mal. 3:3 . . . "He shall sit as a refiner and purifier of silver. He shall purge the priesthood of the people that they may offer unto the Lord an offering in righteousness." Islam comes to

The Honorable Mr. Elijah Muhammad

reform the so—called Negro and to save him from God's destruction of the enemy devil. *(Our Saviour Has Arrived pg. 142)*

The Will of Allah must be done. Allah, through His Will, will come out Himself to be the champion and lead the righteous to Victory. His Will shall not be hindered by anyone. *(Our Saviour Has Arrived pg. 145)*

I think that there are many meaningful Black professional people who could, if they would, unite with me and my Followers and the whole picture of America would change at once. With the Help of Allah (God), we will not fail. Allah (God) Will Not Let us fail. But we need the sure Friendship of a friend that will not fail us in the time of trouble. For this is the time of trouble in which we are living. *(Our Saviour Has Arrived pg. 150)*

In the Bible, Rev. 14:1, we find the Lamb (Messenger of Allah, God) standing on the Mount Zion (foreign shore); with him was a hundred and forty four thousand (his followers who had escaped from the anger of the beast). *(Our Saviour Has Arrived pg. 162)*

The fleeing out of Jerusalem under the cover of darkness is backed up by prophecy made in the Bible, Ez. 34:12, " . . . and will deliver them out of all places where they have been scattered in the cloudy and dark day." This is referring to the last days; that Allah (God) would gather us in under a cover of a

The Future Master Fard Muhammad

cloudy and dark day. We go further back to prophecy. Bible Ex. 12:31,42 says that Israel was brought out of Egypt under cover of darkness. The Bible, Rev. 8:12 refers to a time of darkness in which "the third part of the sun, moon and stars was smitten and it was dark part of the day and the night." *(Our Saviour Has Arrived pg. 163)*

And there is no such thing as your worshipping Jesus on the 25th of December. He was a righteous prophet of God, 2,000 years ago, and they disgrace this righteous prophet and his name by worshipping a false day that he was not even born on. And the material they use to worship the Jesus is drinking whisky, beer, wine, and fighting, gambling, doing all acts of evil on that day. When I was a little boy coming up, the men folk would think that there were not taking Christmas unless they had plenty of liquor and whisky to drink and they would get half drunk and vomit all over the streets and highways. It is a sin and disgrace to be calling yourself worshipping a righteous person and celebrating his birthday with all kinds of drinking and gambling. This shows you that this was not the Jesus' birthday because if you acted like this on the real birthday of the righteous, the God would punish you. You do not get away with mistreating the righteous and not be punished. The evil people have a time to flourish in evil doings to do all kinds of evil until the end of their time which is now. That evil will be punished in the day of the God

The Honorable Mr. Elijah Muhammad

of Justice and Righteousness. You will read that righteous people, even to prophets, were killed by the white race, Jews, and some of those who killed the prophets were not destroyed because it was the time that evil was to triumph over the righteous. Now, today is the day of Allah (God) and His World Will Be a world of Righteousness, Freedom, Justice and Equality. And we cannot get away with falsehood in His Day and Time and in the building up of His Kingdom without being punished immediately. *(Our Saviour Has Arrived pg. 180—181)*

The prophecy of the coming of the Son of Man and the days of the Son of Man is almost the whole of the Bible, scriptures, histories and prophecies. The people who read the Bible should understand these things. You should want to read and understand.

Let us see what and who is the Son of Man who is mentioned here. We are all sons of some man, but this specifies the Son of Man coming in the Last Days to Judge man.

True understanding and the answers to these questions destroy any mistaken ideas or misunderstandings and prophecies of the Bible and Holy Qur'an concerning the coming of the Son of Man.

The true knowledge of Who is the Son of Man and Why He is Called the Son of Man destroys the teachings of the Christians concerning the prophecies of the Son of Man and the coming of the Son of Man.

The Future Master Fard Muhammad

This forces understanding upon the world that is blind to the knowledge of Who and Why He is Called the Son of Man . . . especially the once slave of the white slave—masters. *(Our Saviour Has Arrived pg. 182)*

The Son of Man, Spoken of as Coming in the Last Days, is the Son of Original Man. Therefore they have it right when they say He is the Son of Man . . . that is the Original Man, the Black man. *(Our Saviour Has Arrived pg. 183)*

The Days of the Son of Man represent the Days (Years) that He Will Be Judging the world and punishing the world for her evil. The Son of Man is gathering, teaching, and training His People right in the midst of this wicked world. His People have gotten experience of the wicked world and He Teaches them how now to avoid the wicked world and its teachings and yet live in the midst of it. Their living in the midst of the evil world and yet avoiding it proves their worthiness since they have gotten experience living in the evil world and now they turn to righteousness while they are still in the midst of the evil world. These people have an experience of both evil and good. Then if these are brought out of the evil world, these people are the people that he said he Saved out of the Fire. The Holy Qur'an says that we were on a Brink of Fire.

The Son of Man . . . the Bible is specific in its prophecy concerning this man. It tells us that we

The Honorable Mr. Elijah Muhammad

should make no mistake for there is no other prophecy of anything other than a Man coming and judging us. We all have been preaching of the day of the Son of Man. The mistaken idea that God is a spook or spirit is due to that which was added by you and your enemy while all the time He is telling you that He is The Son of Man.

The Great Mahdi, the Saviour of His People . . . Bible Mt. 1:21 prophesied that He Was Born to Save His People from sin. They were guilty of the same sin as that of their evil teacher, for they practiced the same sin.

Upon the coming of God, the Son of Man, He being the Just Judge of Man and man—kind, He forgave us our sins because we are not guilty of that which we did not know. *(Our Saviour Has Arrived pg. 184—185)*

In the Days of the Son of Man there will be much trouble and confusion of Nations. Bible Is. 2.24:1 says the whole earth will be turned upside down and nations scattered abroad. The Bible says (Mt. 25:32) "Before Him shall be gathered all nations." The Holy Qur'an says, "you shall see all nations kneeling before Him and they shall be judged out of their own books." The government keeps a record of their governmental accounts. They have books in the library and in the courts which tell how they have ruled the people. They have a record of how they have judged the people.

The Future Master Fard Muhammad

The Holy Qur'an says that God will Judge them out of their own books which have the condemnation of their own evil and unjust judgment which they did give out to the people, especially the poor Black slave.

Boom, that is the end when this is accomplished. When the Son of Man proves that He is Justified in destroying the wicked, then they will be destroyed in the twinkling of an eye. *(Our Saviour Has Arrived pgs. 185—186)*

As Jesus was not of the world of the white man, so are we of the world of the white man. And the parable that he put before you prophesies how God would come, searching for you to take you out of the world of the wicked, and put you into your own world of Peace and security. Also see Bible (Ez. 34, Bible). *(Our Saviour Has Arrived pg. 194)*

The Real God and Owner of the earth Comes In Angry like a man who returns home and finds someone in his house who has destroyed his house and his best furniture and who has beat—up those whom the Real Owner has left among the erstwhile owner.

The Bible prophesies of the Coming of God with Anger. He is very Angry against the evil people and He is Ready to Destroy them from the face of the earth! *(Our Saviour Has Arrived pg. 196)*

Therefore, Allah (God) has to Strike both parties, the white man (devil) and the Black, blind, deaf and

The Honorable Mr. Elijah Muhammad

dumb lovers of their enemy, with a severe chastisement, in order to open their blind eyes, as he did in Jesus' parable of the rich man and the poor man, Lazarus (Bible Luke 16:19—25). Lazarus refused to give up begging his master for survival until Allah (God) sent a famine on the rich man. The worse famine that man has ever seen is prophesied to come upon America. *(Our Saviour Has Arrived pg. 199)*

The God of Freedom, Justice, and Equality desires to take over in His time, and not before. This is His Time to remove the burden of suffering and mistreatment under the law of their own courts from the shoulders of the people.

He desires to set up a government without this type of court (christian) which claims to be the courts of justice, but on examining their decisions, we find that the christian courts are courts of injustice. *(Our Saviour Has Arrived pg. 205)*

PART IV

The Future Master Fard Muhammad

How to Eat to Live
(Book 1 and 2)

See Isaiah 66:18: "For I know their works and their thoughts: it shall come, that I will gather all nations and tongues; and they shall come, and see my glory."

The glory means the right way that He will teach the people in the last days; that He will approve of our doing what He gives to us in the Resurrection. He knows your works that ignore His law of righteousness, given to His prophets of old, and your self—centered thoughts, or your thinking that you can deceive others, while breaking the law of God, into thinking you are right in eating the swine. But, He has promised death to you in the 17th verse. He will consume such people all together. *(How to Eat to Live Book 1 pg. 98)*

The Honorable Mr. Elijah Muhammad

Since the white race is more guilty than anyone else of breaking the law of Allah (God), He threatens with chastisement and total destruction. We may quote Isaiah 65:15. It reads like this: "And ye shall leave your name for a curse unto my chosen; for the Lord God shall slay thee (the disobedient white race), and call his servants by another name."

Here we are warned that God will not accept us in the name of the white race, because He has another name that He will call us by, and He mentions this throughout Isaiah and the New Testament. We must have a name of God and not the name of an enemy of God. *(How to Eat to Live Book 1 pg. 99)*

In order to lengthen our lives, we must begin with what we put in us that retains life. Master Fard Muhammad, to Whom Praises are due forever, comes to prolong the lives of the believers. *(How to Eat to Live Book 2 pg.13)*

Master Fard Muhammad, to Whom Praises are due forever, comes to prolong our lives, not to shorten them, by correcting our eating habits to one meal a day instead of three, and by teaching us to eat the proper foods that will not destroy us or shorten our lives to less than 100 years.

His (Allah's) teaching us to eat better food and to cut our eating from three and four times a day to once a day will certainly prolong our lives and increase our beautiful appearance. *(How to Eat to Live Book 2 pg.14)*

The Future Master Fard Muhammad

Eat to live and not to die. The Bible teaches us that God, in the end of the world when He comes, will prolong the people's lives because they have been eating the proper foods, both spiritually and physically. We have to accept it——that is, if we love life and not death. *(How to Eat to Live Book 2 pg. 21)*

If you will stop eating foods such as sugar and starchy foods, I know you will do better. I have been self experienced in everything, and I have been a victim of everything that you are a victim of, except cancer. I do not think that I have cancer; but as I mentioned in this book before, The Last Messenger is not immune to the sickness and complaints of the common people. He is also to suffer; but yet, as the Book says, the Pleasure of the Lord is with him and that in His Own Good Time, He Will Heal all of us. *(How to Eat to Live Book 2 pg. 27)*

I suffer sickness with you. I suffered imprisonment with you. I suffered the deprivation of family as you have. Show me what you have suffered, that I have not suffered. It is necessary for the Last Messenger to suffer a taste of what all of the prophets before him suffered. Therefore, the Last Messenger is called the fulfillment of the prophets. He fulfills the same history of the former prophets . . . except death. He is not to be murdered . . . God Will Not Suffer that. *(How to Eat to Live Book 2 pg. 69)*

The Honorable Mr. Elijah Muhammad

When I was in Phoenix, Arizona, a few years ago, before I arrived someone had fired shots at my house. Another devil said, "Do not shoot him, get him in his water." What had I done to be shot or poisoned for? That shows that they are the murderers of the prophets of old, and that Allah (God) Should Take revenge on this generation for the righteous that they killed before. *(How to Eat to Live Book 2 pg. 70)*

Since God Almighty has given us the truth — the spiritual truth — then He (Allah) must give us physical guidance to protect the life of the spiritual truth. *(How to Eat to Live Book 2 pg. 31)*

If the medical doctors and the theologian teachers and scientists of chemicals, are indulging and are not successful expanding their own lives in what they are offering to us to eat and drink, then why should we follow their way of life? The chemical doctors go to the earth to get chemicals to heal themselves and us. These chemicals soon will destroy both. And, their bodies were not made to be supported by chemicals for health and longevity.

The fact is the body of man was not to be drugged. This white man brought all this "stuff" on us, because he was not going to be righteous, and he went to the earth to try to find a 'god' for his belly in drugs and chemicals. Now the 'thing' is catching up with him with what his own hands have produced. And they are willing to confess that these things are not good for us. They are turning down much of their

The Future Master Fard Muhammad

medication, which is absolutely poison and detrimental to us. It is prophesied in the Holy Qur'an that when God of Truth, Freedom, Justice, and Equality Comes, He Will Force this evil world to confess their evil. And, this, they are doing. *(How to Eat to Live Book 2 pg.158)*

DO YOU THINK the old patriots who lived 500, 600, 700, 800, 900 and nearly 1,000 years ate such filth? What do you think they ate? They did not eat your pig. They did not gobble down all kinds of meats and other foods three times a day. Some of them did not eat but one or two times a whole week. How do you think the people on Mars lived? "I do not know," you will say. And, they lived twelve hundred of our earth years. The Bible teaches us, and it is supposed to be from Jesus, that when God Comes, He comes to bring you life and take away death and give you more of abundance, plenty. He cannot do it without regulating our eating habits. So, this is the way to live a long time. *(How to Eat to Live Book 2 pg. 159)*

The Honorable Mr. Elijah Muhammad

PART V

The Future Master Fard Muhammad

The Theology of Time

The old Christianity, the doom of the black man, this is the thing that dooms you. The knowledge of it will save you. That cross represents their blood thirst for death of righteous human beings. All throughout your Bible they were after prophets who would come among them preaching the truth. Some they beat up, jailed, and some they killed. I am the last of those righteous reformers. I'm the last one. Your Bible teaches you that, and I will prove it to you if you come and listen. There is no need for a prophet to come after me, why? Because I bring you face to face with God and man.

He swung the righteous from the cross he made, following him was his people. Hung high in the limbs of trees for his body to be riddled with bullets from the Christian guns. So we are here sent from God, Himself, having the power from God to put an end to

The Future Master Fard Muhammad

it. My work is to put an end to it, and by Allah, we will do it. Christianity, what is Christ? What does Christ mean? What is the real truth of the meaning of Christ? It means one coming in the last days to crush the world of evil. Christ is a crusher. You don't get that name in the Bible until his time, then you read of Christ coming. He's the crusher of this religion: a lying religion, a religion that teaches you must die before you can see the hereafter or the heaven. This is true if you understood what the liar was saying. Sure, you have to die mentally, out of the evil death that he put you in. He teaches you that there is a hereafter after you die, that's right, but after you die the mental death that he put you in from slavery, up until now, until the judgment comes in, then you got to be resurrected totally from the mental death that you died in, not physically.

We the little people in North America, called every name but the true names of ourselves, God will soon give you this whole entire earth and He will begin here in North America. This is the country that He will take and send to its doom, the Honor of it, pretty soon. This the first one, because he acted so brave and in mockery of God and His work. So, He will make him His example for Europe.

He breaks their power to rule. He brings to naught their trade between each other. That's going on now. Never, since you've been born, have you seen a president of this country going over the earth

The Honorable Mr. Elijah Muhammad

to the nations of the earth begging them to agree with him to live longer. He has everything the other nations have, but he knows the other nations have their weapons trained on him, and that he would not last long if he would train his mighty weapons upon the people that are now against him. They will tell you, "We have it, but we're scared to use it," because others have the same. He's pleading with the nations not to use these dreadful destroyers of nations on each other; whereas, we will destroy ourselves if we destroy them.

We can, because, "they have that champion of war with them, the Mahdi," and

He won't allow us to fight the Blackman in such a way to annihilate them from the earth. He told me and taught me about what they would do, our people, those seven angels that you read about in Revelations – what they will do when He starts. They are capable of cutting a corridor in the air between this country and the other countries, confining all of His Destruction in This Sphere. Think over that. *(The Theology of Time; June 4, 1972)*

If we would look into the face of Christianity, as it stands in its Christian practice, I think you ought to put it down, because you don't understand. The first part of it spells Christ. Christ actually means the crusher who's coming in the last day to crush the wicked. It doesn't mean what you think, no. That's

The Future Master Fard Muhammad

the man to rid us of that "—ianity" out there at the end of it.

Who is the Mahdi? He is the God we call Allah. We call Him other names, but

He is the One also Who is referred to in our Bible that will come. Mahdi means a name of self independence, One who doesn't rely on others; He's self independent and He's one that is coming in the last days to bring about the judgment of the made—man. He's referred to by many as being the Son of Man. I don't know whether I should tell you all of this or not? The Son of Man is that man Who is given authority and power by God to carry out His judgment upon the people. That's what Son of Man is. *(The Theology of Time; June 11, 1972)*

There was no man that had come up who had the wisdom of Yakub, to take away His rule until the birth of the Mahdi, Whom I represent to you, in the name of Master Fard Muhammad in person, as the Bible teaches you: You will see God as He is in person in the Judgment. *(The Theology of Time; June 18, 1972)*

We want to tell you what Islam is. This is what you came for. You have never known what Christianity is, although you glorify that it's your religion and that it's Jesus Christ's religion. Jesus Christ never taught Christianity and you can't prove it to me. The "Christ," on the front end of that name, means the Crusher. The plural part of it means that

The Honorable Mr. Elijah Muhammad

which the people believe in. Actually, you are believing in a religion which is not yours. It means, a Crusher coming at the end of their time to crush the people that believe in that kind of religion. Christ definitely means a crusher.

You and I were reared by the devil, in his hell. Since we were reared by the devil, it takes an awful powerful teacher to get him out of you. He claims that his number is the same as ours. It's got to be the same as ours since we made him. He didn't make himself. We made him. The Holy Qur'an teaches us that the God of Islam, called Allah, which is His most proper name, because Allah covers it all, but He being the Supreme One, they distinguish Him by calling Him the Mahdi, an Independent God. He's Self Sufficient. I want you to know this God, of whom the Holy Qur'an teaches us, is coming in the last day – according to the 22nd Surah [chapter] of the Qur'an, with the name "Mahdi." It means He's Self—independent.

The original creator was only allowed to keep just a little, just a spark, to keep from going out of the time. The Holy City Mecca had this little spark. This Holy City Mecca of Arabia, the original scientist didn't rule there, nor do they rule there today, but they're gradually easing in. There are white scientists who's ruling there. This is why Muhammad must destroy the old. You find in the history of Muhammad that he destroyed the old. You find in the

The Future Master Fard Muhammad

history of Muhammad that he declared war on Mecca and he overcame them. So today, I'm telling you that we are not going to fight to become the ruler under the same thing that the old world has ruled under. We're going to make our own Holy City. You'll read in the Bible where it says that, "I saw a new Jerusalem coming down from out of the throne of God – the new God. He has a new city. He won't let His New Wisdom and His New Kingdom be built upon an old foundation. *(The Theology of Time; June 25, 1972)*

It's seven of them. Allah says that the job is not enough for one, but seven of them will be ordered to do it. And think over it, these are not spooks, they are men. Last of all is that dreadful angel which places one foot on land and one on sea. That's the dreadful one, that's the 7th one. The book says and Allah affirmed it, he lifted up his right hand and his left hand to heaven. This is the way Muslims pray. They lift up their hands and they pray like that, both hands. He said in his words, "Time, time, [as we] know it now will soon know no more," He then cuts a shortage into gravity and sets the nation on fire. This cutting a shortage means cutting a shortage into the atom of the gravity of earth and make the atom over the earth explode. When they explode, they set all the atmosphere into a flame of fire and there is no people that can live on the earth, because it all will be in a flame of fire. This is the way the heavens and the

The Honorable Mr. Elijah Muhammad

earth will be displayed, as the Judgment of the Bible teaches you. The flame will only go up 12 miles high, but it will most certainly get you who are on the earth, if you don't get with Allah. *(The Theology of Time; July 9, 1972)*

The stock market tells you what your money's doing, it's dying. I begged you in 1970 to loan me your money and that I would pay you ten cent on the dollar, but you think your great god, the devil, has plenty of money and, *"I will give it to him and let him pay me interest on it."* Pretty soon, he won't be getting any himself, nor you. There will come a time, I want you to remember that I'm not dumb to it, that he will come out making you to believe that he has a great future. God will fool him like that, to get you like He did all the other great strong people that He destroyed. He gave them a little break before their actual death.

We have it written in the book [Bible] that, "As it was in the day of Noah so shall it be in the day of the Son of Man." *"Who is the Son of Man Mr. Muhammad?"* We all are sons of men brother, but this Son of Man is different from all the other sons. The God that I call your attention to today, is a Son of Man. You use to hear this from the Christian pulpit and you had to use your imagination about that Son of Man. What that actually means is that the God who has the power to bring in the Judgment over the made man, also is a made man and the Son of the

The Future Master Fard Muhammad

Real man. I know, if I was in the church, they'd throw me out, because they don't understand. He is the Son of Man to usher in the Judgment and judge man; yet He is a made—man too.

You're reading books of how he has destroyed and continues to destroy you. You have lots of books teaching you today. He's putting them out himself of how he poisoned the Blackman in his food, water, and in his medicine. He's poisoned it. He especially doesn't want to leave his black slaves here whom he taught from the cradle. Now, for God to take that same man, of whom it is written that the devil taught, He will teach him the wisdom of how to rid the Earth of him [the devil]. This is what you must remember: Bear in mind at all the times that Jehovah did not drown Pharaoh; He made Moses do the job. Over in the Bible, Revelations, He did not sound the trumpet Himself, but He made an angel do it. He told the angel where to go and how to stand. You must remember how to understand the Theology of God's teaching; you must understand. *(The Theology of Time; July 30, 1972)*

The Bible teaches you that the devil will have power to rule over the people until God comes and destroy them. This is true. God prepared hell for him in the day that he was made. Think over that. Before the man was ever made, hell was prepared for him. If the Bible teaches you that, Christian believers, why do you want to go along with him, since his

The Honorable Mr. Elijah Muhammad

destination is hell. You say, "*I don't know when that will be, neither do you.*" No one is given that hour but God Himself and then He passes it over to that angel that you read of in the Revelation that places one foot on water and one on land.

The preachers use to use their imagination in that. Of course, they didn't get too far from the truth. They use to say that the angel would ask God, "*How loud was the sound?*" He'd make it a little imaginary. I use to hear my father preach it and he'd put his imagination to it, because he didn't know. Today all imagination is removed and the light of truth must shine so clear that you cannot claim that there was a cloud between you and it. I am the little boy that's talking to you now. There is no body coming behind me but God. I'd better tell you that.

I'm like it's written in the Bible; wherein, it says that, "*Before that great and dreadful day, I will send you Elijah and . . . he shall prepare the way.*" He must have enough converts to lay claim to the devils world, because God would have some people in it. We can't execute Judgment on the enemy until we separate them. We must separate the enemy from the righteous. The first thing He did is call all us righteous. How did He do that? You follow Satan and all that you do of evil, you've gotten it from Satan. Now, Satan is to be destroyed and God has come to take that which is not Satan's and give him his own. How are we going to escape? It's plain and easy to

The Future Master Fard Muhammad

separate you by what you do if you are following after the devil.

God comes and declares that you are not one of the devils and that you are now the righteous. You say, *"I haven't been righteous."* No you haven't. That which you were, unrighteous, it was not your character, that was the devil's. You had no teacher to argue with the devil and his teaching, which caused us to act contrary to our nature. We are not devils by nature. We had been deceived by the devil and didn't know who he was. We didn't have any teacher of our own to tell us to, *"come back, don't follow that man."* He kept our foreign visitors away from us. When they came in the country, he kept them among himself and we never saw any of them or knew they were here. We didn't know ourselves.

Allah didn't come here to make us ugly. He didn't come here to let us remain ugly. Every one accepts Him, He starts you to growing into a new life. That growth is a beautiful person. I'm your teacher. The Holy Qur'an teaches us that if you who turn to righteousness in this day and time, at the end of the Caucasian's world, Allah will make you grow into a new growth. He told me about it when He was with me. He said, *"No brother, we will have no ugly people. We will have no people with gray hair and bald heads . . . "* He said, *"Brother, all of our black hair will come back to us."* And the Holy Qur'an says this is done by Him blessing the righteous in

The Honorable Mr. Elijah Muhammad

growing into a new growth instead of you growing and aging up into decay, decay stop on the other side, no more decay. *(The Theology of Time; August 6, 1972)*

Behold, I make all things new. This is what the scripture prophesied of God, that for the first time, you will witness seeing Him in person. All in the past, except with Moses, the God was not seen in person, because it would bring about a change. The change was not to come in those days, that would have been a permanent change; therefore, you and I are lucky to be living here today to see the God that will set up the kingdom of Islam to live forever without any future interference. There never will be an enemy openly attacking Islam, the religion of truth, and righteousness anymore. There is no future prophesy of any. This is the end of opposition and attacks against the righteous and their religion of Islam.

We have been told all of our lives that a Judgment would come and that God will judge both truthful and untruthful. We find in the Holy Qur'an where the author of other than truth try denying misleading us and that he will declare himself a believer in what Allah has brought to us like crazy Pharaoh. He waited until he was near drowning to death before he would admit Allah was the Greatest. That didn't help him much. He had to drown just the same, but to show you that Allah is All Merciful, He

The Future Master Fard Muhammad

gave him a break for just saying He was the Greatest, because Pharaoh had tried to make himself greatest. When he had no mastery over the water that was taking his life from him, he said, "Allah U Akbar, Allah U Akbar," You're the Greatest, You're the Greatest. Allah gave him credit for admitting He was the Greatest.

Let Thy Will be done, as it is in heaven, let it be done on earth. Your Will shall not be hindered by no means and by no one. Therefore, God raises up Himself to fight the war for truth, peace and security for the righteous. He comes out Himself to be the champion, and leads the righteous to victory. It is a great thing to know that His Will comes into practice and use, in the last days, wherein, God only Wills it and there it is, This is the way it began at the beginning.

The Bible teaches you and me that this Elijah must first come. He doesn't come after God. He goes before God, and this is what the book means. He must first come, but right behind him God will appear.

The Will of God, "*Let Thy Will be done.*" The Christians pray " . . . *on Earth as it is in heaven.*" But, you and me never did get the true meaning of what he meant. How can Thy Will, meaning Allah's Will, be done as long as the will of the devil is practiced? You cannot set up the Will of God universally as long as He has a free enemy to attack

The Honorable Mr. Elijah Muhammad

His Will. We must rid the people of the open enemy, as the Holy Qur'an teaches, from attacking the truth and from attacking the truthful ones. We must rid the Earth of such opponents, who are not secret. They are open opponents. We must rid the Earth of open enemies and secret enemies.

According to the teachings of Allah to me, North America is that lake of fire. Not Michigan, but the lake is on the Earth of North America. The atoms will be exploded and set afire everything that is on this "Earth" of North America. He said to me, that it will burn for 390 years, close to the time that they have kept us here. It was near 400 years that they kept us in servitude slavery. So, Allah will burn them for that length of time. He's just that angry with them for destroying us, and then making enemies of His people, against Him. *(The Theology of Time; August 20, 1972)*

He knows Malcolm was not with me, so he gets you to worship hypocrites of Elijah Muhammad, so that you'll go to hell with them. My God has struck out after you a hundred percent. When He does, you won't go to hell with them. You're going to remember this talk, and you're going to come back to Elijah and shake my hand and say, *"Mr. Muhammad, I'm with you."* I know you're going to do that. I don't care what you believe in now. You can believe in Buddhism; it doesn't make any difference to me.

The Future Master Fard Muhammad

There's a set time when Allah's going to make you to bow to Him!

There is nothing in divine that you can ask of me that I cannot answer, but you get up something else, that's different. If it's divine, I am here to teach you the knowledge of Him and what He's about to do in setting up His Will, as the Christian call it, the Kingdom of God on Earth. This is what I'm here to teach you. What His Will is about to do for you and me. If you think that is not enough, well there's plenty of people who are studying other types of work and professions. Maybe they'll answer you in their way or according to their learning, but I am a divine teacher and what I answer is of divine. *(The Theology of Time; August 27, 1972)*

I want the Christian preachers to listen to all I have to say, then you ask me anything that I don't make clear to you, to make it clearer. Since you are a student and preachers of the scripture, then you ought to know me, because the Bible prophesies of Elijah coming to you and I am Elijah. This man prophesies and the Bible teaches you that he must first come. He must first come, meaning, he must come before God to make a way for God to come.

If that man has to come first, not God coming first, but He must send this man first, then He comes after this man. What is this man and what and why is he so important that he must go ahead of God? He must prepare the way. Why doesn't God prepare the

The Honorable Mr. Elijah Muhammad

way? Why should he send Elijah to prepare the way? Because, He prepared Elijah to prepare the way. This is done by governments, and nations all over the Earth. They send an ambassador to a foreign nation, to get acquainted with that nation so that the king, president or the people of a foreign land may get friends with each other. I'm here to get you acquainted with God, so that we can see whether or not you're able to live with God after your acquaintance. *(The Theology of Time; September 3, 1972)*

He's angry with the wicked world and so am I. As it is written, they both were angry, for the wrath had come. It was time to get angry, because the enemy was trying to prevent the dead from rising. God and His Messenger are here for that exact purpose. It is to see that they rise, regardless to opposition. They must rise. God intends to make a new nation out of us, not to keep us like we are now. Some may say, *"Where are we going?"* We don't need to go no place. Hell is made by the people and not by the nature of our reactionary Earth. We make the hell and we make Heaven. What is hell? It's a place where people are disagreeable to live with in peace. Heaven is a peaceful place where people live in peace. Every man would like to enjoy peace, though he breaks the peace and contentment in the community, he would like a contented place for himself. My God and myself, we want to see about

The Future Master Fard Muhammad

all of that. *(The Theology of Time; September 10, 1972)*

I don't like to criticize anyone, because this is not what we are after today. We don't want to criticize each other. We can get together and squash that thing called criticizing. In fact, that's what Islam has come for: to put a stop to Black men making fun of Black men. Islam is here to make us brothers, and if we can't be brothers, we're here to push him out of the circle. God Himself is here for the purpose of showing you and me that which will help us and do for us. If we can't, He's here to push us in the lake, and not a lake of water, it's a lake of fire. That's what He's ready to do for us.

We want to get together here in America first of all, and build us something of our own that the world will recognize. There is no work going on in America that you can compare with our workers. No worker has the progress as our workers. They don't enjoy progress. I don't care where you're from, brother and sister, you are the best. We are able to get the confidence of the nations of the Earth. They will help us in every way that we call on them. They will do it. God will make them do it. We are with God and God is with us.

Allah will remove the modern made religion called Christianity. The very foundation of that religion is murder. Take a look at the cross. It's the sign of a murder. If you will follow a murderer for

The Honorable Mr. Elijah Muhammad

life, what life could he give you if he's a murderer? He put up his sign for you and I to worship. If we're going to worship a sign of a murderer or worship a murderer, then what are we looking for? Death. We are looking for death. *(The Theology of Time; September 17, 1972)*

We want you to know that the Islamic believers are now in for building a world of their own. They are not satisfied with this world and we are trying to build a world of our own. We don't have to try much, for the world is already carved out by divine; therefore, it stops us from trying to carve out pictures trying to make a world. The world is already carved out for us and the Architect is Allah, Himself. I don't think you have much to argue with.

That man spoken of in the beginning of the book is spoken of as straightening up the old path and making way for God to come to the people. He makes a path and then your Lord, your God, Whom you wish to see, will come suddenly after Elijah makes a path for Him. The path is too crooked for God to come on. Elijah must come in and make some followers. This is what they call the pathway. He's got to have something of His own to come after. All He wants you to do is just give Him a chance to claim you, so He can fight the enemy that has held you in the bondage of sin. So the book teaches us that Elijah must come and make a way for his God to come and get His people. Elijah just made a few

The Future Master Fard Muhammad

people, so that God could have a claim on the whole. This is wonderful. Elijah straightens out the world of his people with just a few. Immediately, here comes the owner of all.

You that follow me, you are the same. You don't fear no evil, because you have Allah on your side. We are a most happy and worthy people for God to choose us to be His people, and will kill nations for you. Your Bible teaches you that, He will destroy nations for your lives, and He's doing it. Why shouldn't we fly to a God like that? *"I've been following Mr. blue—eyed Caucasian all my life and I have come to love him. I wishes to kill your God and my God to save him."* Oh brother, that's bad. That's just what you say in your heart. I wish they didn't exist. I would kill them if I could. *(The Theology of Time; September 24, 1972)*

We have, as you know, our program which is, doing something for yourself. If God will give you and me the kingdom, we have to learn how to keep up the kingdom. If you give a man something and he doesn't know how to keep it up, you're wasting time. We must learn how to keep it up. As the Bible teaches us, that you're raised up to rebuild the wasted cities; that's here in your Bible, so those who will waste the cities are the ones, out of whose way, we want to stay. They will be causing trouble. I'm looking for capable people to help me put this job over and put it over at once.

The Honorable Mr. Elijah Muhammad

There is no other Messenger or prophet coming after me. I'm the last one of those kind of people. No Warner will ever come after me. The only Warner that will come after me is that One of Whom you read about in the Bible; wherein it says, "He went and placed one foot on the sea, one on the side of land, lifted up a trumpet and his words were, "The time as you know it you will soon know no more." That man will have his foot in those positions, because he's going to cut a shortage in gravity, so Allah taught me. We had read it, but we didn't know how He was going to bring it about. He said the way He will do it, is cut a short in the gravity like a shortage in these electric wires in the wall. When he does that, all the air over land will burst into flame of fire and the water will not burst with fire, but land only. These flames will leap up into space 12 miles – they will be that high – nothing but a flame of fire burning the atmosphere. The atmosphere that you breathe will become a flame of fire.

I'm not raised around here just to keep you company, but I'm raised up by Almighty God to do just what you find in the Bible, the parable concerning God raising up someone to teach you; I'm that fellow. I am the Bible's Elijah that must come. That man, according to the Bible, he must precede God himself, to make a way for God. What is this way? It is to convert people of God that believe in the God Whom we are expecting to present Himself to

The Future Master Fard Muhammad

us. This man must have a knowledge of that God must know that God, so he can teach you what you may expect to be arriving soon; he knows that. God acquaints him with that God first. *(The Theology of Time; October 22, 1972)*

PART VI

The Future Master Fard Muhammad

The True History of Elijah Muhammad

You also have been taught that he rose up the third day, after being buried like all other men. That is science and that science you have never known. The secret of that is your own self here in America. Not that Jesus two thousand years ago was buried some place and he rose again after the third day. That third day, that three days that he was in the earth, it means none other than you and a Saviour coming after you.

It means this: that Jesus being buried — that name Jesus means Justice there — and that you have been buried here in the midst of the enemy, the white man, away from all of your people for three hundred years. You were here without any contact with any of your people just as though you were over here dead. After three hundred years in the four hundredth year, God would come to you and would revive you into

The Future Master Fard Muhammad

the knowledge of yourself and resurrect you into the knowledge of yourself and you will return to your own home and to your own people in the four hundredth year. That's what it means. *(The True History of Elijah Muhammad pg. 2)*

After a certain year God will return again, and when He returns, that will be the end of the world. He will gather all those that believed and followed that Messenger to whom He revealed Himself. He won't return to teach you. No, but will come after that people that believed in the word that He communicated to His Messenger. *(The True History of Elijah Muhammad pg. 3)*

As it is written and I believe it, "*Behold, the Son of Man cometh*. The Son of Man. I believe in the Son of Man, but I don't believe in no son of a spook. I don't believe spirits can produce me a son, but I do know a man and a woman can.

According to the Bible, in the Revelation, it prophesies that there is a wonder in heaven. Let's see now where is this son coming from in the last day. *"And I saw a great wonder in the heaven, a woman clothed with the sun, and the moon under her feet and upon her head a crown of twelve stars." (The True History of Elijah Muhammad pg. 3)*

Here, the woman is seen a long time before she gives birth to such a child. She was seen six thousand years before the birth of that child. She was seen among the Holy people carrying a child. Who's

The Honorable Mr. Elijah Muhammad

government was going to be like the sun. Carrying a child who's government or his teachings or his religion, as you would call it, would be as clear as the sun and that his truth, his government, his religion would block out or make the old religious world or the old religious teaching vanish, as the day sun blocks out the light of the moon. And the old world, or the old prophets' dispensation, they would become like the moon. *(The True History of Elijah Muhammad pg. 6)*

I want you to understand your book. It's beautiful, if you understand it. It's just like playing with rattlesnake poison if you don't understand it. I say my friend, this is the wilderness of your Bible, it's America. The beast that will destroy the child is none other than the white man. The woman fled in the wilderness where she had a place. Until what? Until the power of the beast has been broken. The Bible don't teach you that. It don't say the power of the beast, but she must flee from the beast for a time and time and a halftime, until the power of the beast is broken. And then at that time, she will have her child walking. *(The True History of Elijah Muhammad pg. 8)*

After Venus or Jupiter or the morning star rises, then you don't need no more stars to rise after that star, because the sun is going to rise. About two hours or a little better than two hours or even less sometimes, the sun is rising. That's the last one there.

The Future Master Fard Muhammad

Your Bible is written pretty good if you understand it. Elijah, it says, is the last one and behind Elijah, it says, the Lord whom you seek will suddenly come. Jesus was here two thousand years ago. It didn't say as soon as Jesus is dead and rose again you will see the Lord. But after Elijah, or rather while Elijah is yet preaching comes the Lord. *(The True History of Elijah Muhammad pg.13)*

I'm like it's written there in the Bible, wherein it says, "Before that great and dreadful day I will send you Elijah and . . . he shall prepare the way." He must have enough converts to lay claim to the devil's world that God would have some people in it. We can't execute judgment on the enemy until we separate them; separate the enemy from the righteous. So the first thing He did is call all us righteous. How did He do that? You follow Satan and all you do of evil, you've gotten it from Satan, now Satan is to be destroyed and God has come to take that which is not his and give him his own. Now how are we going to escape? It's plain, what you would do if you were following after him — the devil. God comes and declares you to be, not one belonging to the devils, but one of the righteous. You say, "I haven't been righteous;" no you haven't. That which you were was unrighteous; it was not yours, that was the devil's, his world. You had no teacher to argue with the devil. The works that he has caused us to do, was not our work by nature. We are not devils by

The Honorable Mr. Elijah Muhammad

nature. Being deceived by the devil and not knowing who he was, we didn't have no teacher of our own to tell us to "come back — don't follow that man." He kept them away from us. When they came in the country, he kept them among himself and we never knew any of them were here, because we didn't know ourselves. *(The True History of Elijah Muhammad pg.16)*

Yes sir. That man spoken of in the beginning of the book almost, he's spoken of as straightening up the old path and making a way for God to come to the people. He will make a path and then your Lord, your God, whom you wish to see, will come suddenly after Elijah picks up a path for Him. The pass is too crooked for God to come in. Elijah must come in and make some followers. This is what they call the pathway. He's got to have something of His own to come after. All He wants you to do is just give Him a chance to claim you, so He can fight the enemy that has held you in the bondage of sin. So the book teaches us that Elijah must come and make a way for his God to come and get His people. Elijah just wakes a little people so that God could have a claim on the whole. This is wonderful. Elijah straightens out the world of his people with just a few, and immediately, here comes the owner of all. *(The True History of Elijah Muhammad pg. 23)*

I warn you of these things, that this is the way that you are traveling now. Allah revealed to me that

The Future Master Fard Muhammad

you will not meet with nothing of good. He shall visit you and your own children with poverty and death. Believe me or wait until it comes to you, it shall soon come. He's very swift in taking retribution against the enemies and hypocrites of His Messenger Elijah Muhammad, as I have warned you of these things. So I say to you who are reading this in Chicago, I Elijah Muhammad is the Messenger of Allah and have proven it to you for over 40 long years. Leave me alone if you don't like me and my followers; leave us alone. Leave us to our God, Allah, to judge us if we are wicked and are false preachers and teachers of His truth. Leave us alone lest you are bound to run into a fire and a very hot fire at that, as He has said, and He will do it. That grievous fire that comes up to the throat, that regretting fire, that hatred of yourself for your own evil doing and sayings, shall come to you and visit you, and you won't be able to close your door against it; it shall come to you whether the door is open or closed. *(The True History of Elijah Muhammad pg. 76)*

I say to you who owns no country, who owns no power in no country, you are helpless, you are servants of the American white people. Fly for your life, fly for your life. There must be something done about your ignorance. What should be done about your ignorance to make you or force you to come to the knowledge of God and the knowledge of yourself and your kind? I ask that question, but I will answer,

The Honorable Mr. Elijah Muhammad

chastisement of Almighty God Allah is the only one now who can force you into submission to His Will, and He forces everything of nature to bow to His Will willingly or unwillingly. He also will make the American so—called Negroes bow to His Will, willingly or unwillingly or be punished night and day with such grief that you cannot sleep day or night; such regret for your ignorance and rejection. The submission to the Will of Almighty God Allah is the condition of His salvation for you. You won't be able to sleep nights or day.

This is coming upon the so—called American Negroes who refuse to accept Islam. What do you think Islam really is? What do you think it really is, I repeat? Islam is the true religion of God. It is entire submission to His Will, and any people on earth or individual who doesn't bow in submission to the Divine Supreme Being, that God will not have mercy on their soul. This you should know. This you have been taught, but you don't believe. *(The True History of Elijah Muhammad pg. 109)*

We want you to remember that the dry bones of Ezekiel was a future mentally dead people who must receive the truth that they may live and unite onto their own kind; for this people is dead, out of their own country. They must be returned to their own people and to their own land. God Almighty Himself, by the hands of a prophet or messenger will do this

The Future Master Fard Muhammad

job in the last days. *(The True History of Elijah Muhammad pg. 145)*

The Orthodox Muslims will have to bow to the choice of Allah. Allah will bring about a new Islam. As for the Principles of Belief, they remain the same. There will be no more signs to be watched for the coming of God and the setting up of a new world of Islam. We are seeing this change now and entering into it. The devils oppose this change, and the Orthodox join them in opposing us because of their desire to carry on the old way of Islam. Allah will place those of His choice in authority in the making of the new world, and others must obey whomever He puts in authority or find themselves fighting against the power of whomever they hold to be on their side and in their favor. We must have a new world. We accept for a new nation completely. *(The True History of Elijah Muhammad pg. 185)*

The Twelve major Imams, as they are called in Islam or in the Arab language, they don't have this one's knowledge. This one has a superior knowledge and that the other Twelve minor or the Twenty four elders, as you find them in the last of the book here, casting down their crown to that One that is conquering the beast and is delivering a people from that beast. They bow down to that One and give praise and honor to him. As though they never knew him before. Read it for yourself.

The Honorable Mr. Elijah Muhammad

They say, worthy is he. As though they never saw him before. Then they said that worthy is the lamb. The lamb looked as though he was slain from the foundation of the earth. He was in a bad looking condition, but worthy is he. Why? Because he was the only one that the God would give his secret to, called the Book that he held in His right hand or that which He held within Himself and would not reveal it to no one, but something that was out of heaven: The Prophet or a Messenger, would receive from God that which no other Prophet ever was able to receive. He is the same that the elders called a lamb and he's the same that the Revelations called *'a baby being born in the midst of beasts.'* That's the one. One that is taken from among you, and the God that comes to you is the one that's born in the heaven.

That God also is born of God. He's born of God and becomes God Himself and then He also gives birth to a Messenger or prophet of His own, that is not chosen by the other righteous. He chose his own man. Then He makes the others to bow to His own man like the father of the Caucasian race did in the year 8,400 or in the 9,000th year of our calendar's history when He was producing the white race. He made his man and then made us to bow to him, so will God in the last days: make Him a man and a people out of no people and then make the others to bow down to Him. All praises due to Allah.

The Future Master Fard Muhammad

You are to go on top, not at the bottom, but on top. Well, how are you going to get on top? Don't look at the physical, or rather worldly wealth. Don't look at that. It's the wisdom that God will give you which is superior to the white race and your own people that is in Asia. He will be with you. He will guide you. He will teach you what he didn't teach them. In your Bible it says, *And God Himself was among them.' Your Bible says that God said, 'I will be their God and they shall be my people and I will lead them into the light of truth and they shall know that I am the God and that these are my people.'* (The True History of Elijah Muhammad pgs. 141—142)

He has made me like Himself. Whatever I do and whatever I want done or will — they use the word will, like He Himself — it will come to pass — don't worry. This is just as important as teaching you the knowledge of him — the devil. You're not going to see the God coming down from heaven and stand here beside me and verify it. The only way the verification comes from Him is if I see you continue being contrary to what I'm teaching you of yourself and the Will of God, that Will is in me too, and that if you fail, Allah will let my will be done on you! *(The True History of Elijah Muhammad pg. 246)*

The righteous God coming at the end of the wicked world must establish a world without the resorting to the use of materials of this world. If He was taught to just say that He would use the method

The Honorable Mr. Elijah Muhammad

of mathematics of this world, He would not be recognized as a God able to build a new world and set a new example of mathematics other than that of this world. He's not to take nothing of this world. He will fulfill the prophesy that Isaiah prophesied, that He will burn up both root and branch. *(The True History of Elijah Muhammad pg. 271)*

Brothers and sisters, brother scholars and scientist, religious scholars and scientist are the ones that I am referring to. Muhammad never did say he saw God at no time. Jesus just 700 years before Muhammad, he said that no man had seen God at anytime. This is where you lost the right path and are straying off, when saying that there is no such thing as "I can see God," but you are wrong there. The writer who wrote this can also defend himself, with respect to no man having seen God, at anytime that was coming in the last day, because the book is based upon the coming of a God to usher in the judgment of this world, and it is that God which no man has seen. He would come at the end of this world, see. *(The True History of Elijah Muhammad pg. 274)*

He will also bring a Book for His people. A book that the present world has not as yet seen and the devils (infidels) may not see it nor touch it. It is not the present Holy Qur'an nor Bible, but a Book containing the guidance for the people in the Hereafter. Not of this world, therefore, it is carefully

The Future Master Fard Muhammad

guarded from the eyes and ears of this world. *(The True History of Elijah Muhammad pg. 287)*

If Moses' rod and book were given as a guide for Israel and the gospel God gave to Jesus as a guide and warning to the Christians, and the Holy Qur'an to Muhammad for the Arab world, will God give us (the so—called Negroes) a book as a guide for us? Will He bring it or send it? For those books were for other people and not for us.

If we are in the change of the two worlds (Christianity and Islam), then surely we need a "new book" for our guidance; for those books have served the people to whom they were given. But all or both books are guidance for us all. Yet we must have a new book for the "new change"; that which no eye has seen nor ear has heard, nor has it entered into our hearts what it is like. We know these books, they have been seen and handled by both the good and no good. *(The True History of Elijah Muhammad pg. 289)*

This book, the Holy Qur'an of today and the Bible is to bring us up to the resurrection, the end of this world, but not to take us through the other world, it is not a guidance for that world. Allah will have a new guidance for that world, because that's a new world, do you understand? It's a new people and a new government for that people, and it's called Islam, and the book is called the Holy Qur'an, because the meanings of the name Qur'an is good for

The Honorable Mr. Elijah Muhammad

that book too. Listen good. *(The True History of Elijah Muhammad pg. 292)*

God is the end of what we have in books when He makes his appearance; that's the end of what we have in books. He then must teach His Messenger what He wants him to know from his mouth, because He must move him up into the knowledge of what He intends to build or create. *(The True History of Elijah Muhammad pg. 295)*

PART VII

The Future Master Fard Muhammad

The True History of Elijah Muhammad Messenger of Allah

The Exegesis of The Pilgrimage

I am Elijah of your Bible, I'm your Muhammad of your Holy Qu'ran. Not the Muhammad that was here 1400 years ago, I am the one that the Holy Qur'an is referring to. The Muhammad that was here 1400 years ago was a white man; then they put up a sign of the real Muhammad. It's there in Mecca Arabia, they call it the little black stone.

I looked at it, I made 7 circuits around it, I kissed the little black Stone but I didn't like to kiss it because I knew what it meant. It means that the people will bow to the real black man that is coming up out of an uneducated people who have not the knowledge of the Bible and Holy Qur'an. And that's

The Honorable Mr. Elijah Muhammad

why they made that stone an unhewed stone: he will be uneducated so I was there kissing the sign of myself and I was afraid to tell them that this is me you're talking about here.

So, what you have been told it was told to you to understand. It was not given to you to understand before that time; this is the time that you must know the secret to all truths that has been put in symbolic manner. Now today, the veil must be lifted; and you understand? — If you believe that I'm he, then you are a very lucky man or woman. It is not that I want you to believe and worship me but believe and worship Him whom I teach to you.

Before we ever suffered ourselves, He, Master W. F. Muhammad, our God and Saviour, the Great Mahdi, Almighty God Allah, in Person, suffered persecution and rejection Himself; all for you and for me.

We are now living in the days of the judgment and in the days of a great separation of peoples and nations. This problem of separating you and me from our enemies and placing us in our own land back among our own people and raising the so—called Negroes of America up to our proper place in civilization is their place.

Remember it was Muhammad who found the black stone out of its place and invited the four chiefs from the four divisions to come forward and take hold of each corner of the mantle and lift it into its

The Future Master Fard Muhammad

place. Remember that it was Muhammad with His own hands who guided it into its place. This was a symbol of you and me here today. We need the help of our people who are living in the four major points of our compass to come and help raise us, their dead brothers, and put us back into our own place: in our own nation among our own people in our own native land.

The sign of the pilgrimage to Mecca, the Black Stone, being made, has been going on now for nearly the last 1400 years.

The Holy Qur'an refers to it and the Bible refers to it, but these are signs of the coming of a nation that was hidden and lost, which God Himself would go after in the last days. After finding that nation, choose that nation for Himself and take it and use it as a builder would in selecting stones or a foundation for a substantial building that he intends to build. He want to build it so it could withstand any strong winds or storms throughout eternity or as long as the earth lasts.

Stones from the earth that has good texture and will stand or live as long as the earth, is necessary in building an eternal kingdom upon the earth that will stand forever, which will not be destroyed by any opposition that may arise. These signs are used for it; the sign of a stone.

In Daniel it is referred to and in Jesus' prophesy this people as a stone that the builders rejected, which

The Honorable Mr. Elijah Muhammad

had become the head and the corner. This is none other than the people of whom the builders of civilization has rejected in the past. They will one day become the head and the corner building of a civilization which will supersede and become the strongest and the mightiest and the greatest of all the civilizations and people that ever was before it. This refers to the lost and found members, the original people who are now called the American Negroes. I wish everyone of you who are called Negroes would jump and shout on hearings of this truth of you.

You have the greatest future of anybody who ever lived on the planet earth, if you would only come and submit to Allah and follow me. This you can learn and enjoy, not having to wait a thousand years, not having to wait a hundred years to enjoy it, right now you can begin enjoying the kingdom of heaven; right now! The King of that kingdom is now present, and the King of that Kingdom is now selecting you for the foundation of that Kingdom; therefore He says to you in these words: "Submit to me and I will sit you into heaven at once. Money, good homes — friendship in all walks of life." This is absolutely true as sunshine. There is lots of opposition against you receiving this salvation and enjoying heaven at once while you live from those who would like to see you to continue to live in the most miseries that humans have ever lived in since there was a man on the face of the earth.

The Future Master Fard Muhammad

I'm here as a brother, a friend to you, and one of the first from the resurrection.

I am the very first. I am the first of those who submitted to the Will of God, in the person of Master Fard Muhammad to whom praise is due forever. I am the first. I am he of whom it is written that was dead and now alive. I am he. I am he of whom it is prophesied as the Messenger of God in the last day who is with God in the resurrection of the dead. I am he. Let your ignorant enemy of the righteous and the truth deceive you against these truths, if you want to take such a one for your guide and for your interpreter. You will suffer the torment and hell of this life. The rejection of the Almighty God, today, and His Messenger will get you nothing but hell in this life, not after you are dead, but while you live.

Take for an instance, the pilgrimage to Mecca that has been going on for the last 1400 years. It is only a sign. Even the city itself is only a sign. Even the Kabbah, that mighty sign sitting there clothed with a black veil, is only a sign. The running to and fro between the hills and the ruins, while visiting this, and heard about in that way: depicts Abraham's wife, Haggar with her young son lying there in the heat suffering for water. He and her went in to find water there. She looked at the feet of her child and there was a well bubbling under her feet that would never go dry. It's only a sign of the coming of God and the finding of His people.

The Honorable Mr. Elijah Muhammad

Go into Mecca, making a pilgrimage to that city, as the 22nd Surah says to you and me in the 27th verse: It says to the Messenger here: "Proclaim to men the pilgrimage, they will come to thee on foot and on every lean camel coming from every little part or path." From all over the earth there has been pilgrimages made to this city. It is a sign that one day at the end of this world, the rule of Satan, the Messenger will call people from every direction, from all of the nations of the Blackman. This is the sign of the resurrection; whereas, whenever the real truth of God has been known, and made manifest to the world through the mouth of that Messenger in the resurrection, every human being who is originally of the nation or aboriginal nation of the earth, will come to the knowledge of that One God, the Truth and to the knowledge of that one shepherd or that one Divine Messenger in that day. Everyone will bow in submission to His will. As the Bible refers to it in this beautiful term, that, "Every knee shall bow, every tongue shall confess that He is God — besides He there is no God.

In the ending of the Bible, that last book referred to the Revelation of John, there we have a symbolic picture of God and the Lamb. The Lamb there receives the greatest revelation that any human beings have ever witnessed since the creation of the heavens and earth. He receives it directly from the All Wise God, Himself, a revelation that was denied

The Future Master Fard Muhammad

the angels of heaven and given to a symbolic person symbolized as a sheep, which only depicts the characteristics of that Last Messenger.

The Last Messenger is a person that is despised and rejected. One of those members of that lost and found people, who were rejected and despised by the builders of civilization, now receives the greatest revelation of all time: to place the unwanted, unfit, rejected, despised, trampled, and murdered outcasts of civilization, into the love and mercy of Almighty God. The mercy of Almighty God and His love in making them His choice and His selection of this particular unwanted people, by the civilizations, would cause the nations of the earth to bow into submission for the first time, since the creation of the heavens and the earth, to that One God, and there, be united together as pilgrims. The sign of it represents or rather is a prophesy of the divine unity of the God and the people of ours and the God together.

This doesn't mean divine unity between God and the enemy of God, it means divine unity of that people which is of God, who have not known that they were of God and who have not known that they were of the real members of God.

This is what I want you to learn, today: Today is the call for you to make a Pilgrimage. Not a Pilgrimage to Mecca for you to be sanctified or become a Holy Muslim. This will not make you a Holy Muslim: going to Mecca, making the

The Honorable Mr. Elijah Muhammad

Pilgrimage there. Every so—called Negro in America can go there if he wanted to or if he's able to, but will that make him a divine choice today? No, because this is a new thing coming in: the presence of God.

After 6,000 years of the work of an evil people, who have ruled the nations under evil and deceit, a very deceptive people, a people for whom the righteous labored under. They are a grievous and a very unjust government, who have poured upon the righteous the worst that could be had or a man could labor under. Today the righteous are now called to make the Pilgrimage. Make your last Pilgrimage, not to that particular city, per say, looking for glorification as they have in the past.

People in the past have worked and made the pilgrimage to Mecca and have returned to their people and teachers to teach them of this sign, but I say the American so—called Negros are the end of that sign. A Pilgrimage there (Mecca) will not help him become a great and righteous Muslim, but the bowing down to that Last Messenger, who God raised from the dead of that people, and recognizing him as being the Guide now for the dead or the absolute [one] to give life to that dead nation, bringing them forth to God, is the real Mecca to which they should make Pilgrimage. The finding of this people and the choice of God for this people to be His, and making them the foundation, a stone for building the kingdom of heaven on earth, absolutely

The Future Master Fard Muhammad

is the end of all pilgrimages. The sign will serve no more purpose when it has been fulfilled. Today, it's being fulfilled.

So here is where the Negro, the so—called Negro, the lost and found member of that righteous nation, must first bow and make a circuit. He must first make a self—confession and join the circle that God is making in the West, so he may be recognized in the circle of the East. This is where he must first pull off the old garments; this is where he must first put on a new coat and the new faith it represents. He must change clothes here, change faith, that's all it means; so he may enter into the mercy of Almighty God and see the hereafter, at which point the earth will become a whole Mecca; wherein the nations of this earth, of aboriginal people, will no more go to Mecca to worship there, but everywhere, as the Jesus prophesied that there would be Mosques in their hearts. As he said to the woman there of Israel: "Woman believe me, the hour cometh", which means the doom of this world ". . . when ye shall neither in this mountain . . ." "meaning the government of Israel" . . . no yet at Jerusalem, the capital, worship the Father." "Ye Worship what you know not what; We know what we worship: for salvation is of the Jews." Listen, let us see and understand what he's talking about. Not yet is this the place where ye shall worship, but the time of the doom after that. All men shall not seek to go no certain place, the whole earth

The Honorable Mr. Elijah Muhammad

will be a Mosque. The whole earth will be a mountain of God where men will worship Him in the spirit of truth and sincerity.

All the world of Islam has to learn what has happened here in America. Islam of Muhammad of 1400 years ago served that time. We need a new Islam to serve this day. My mission is to convert all black people on earth into the knowledge of God. Acquaint them all with a new Islam and God. There will be a new world all together.

Allah Guides me to do things like a God. The prophets said, "Thus saith the Lord." I say, "Here is the Lord." I was taught into the wisdom of God, not prophets. I am the end of prophets. The more closer you try to live to me and try to follow me, the more better your life. It is so essential that you follow the Messenger because if you do as I say you become a different person. What Allah has revealed to me is a base for building a universal knowledge. It has not become universal or we would not be preaching. It is to become universal.

I'm charged with delivery of the message, not a one of you is charged with that because the message was given to me and if I have 40 million helpers they all — everyone of them is helping not that they are responsible for the message, if you read the Qur'an and Bible, I'm the only one Allah will hold responsible for you not getting the truth because He gave me the truth and the way He gave it to me, He

The Future Master Fard Muhammad

gave it to me like a flowing spring or like a flowing fountain. The fountain have enough drink in it to give everyone a drink that come to drink. You don't need a new fountain, just try and drink up what this fountain has to drink!

So in the Holy City Mecca there is a well there, call it the well of Zam Zam and . . . that the righteous drinks of this little water, but they shall drink the spiritual truth from Allah from which they will never be able to get to the end of it — it's so much. Now that this sign here is a sign of the truth that the Messenger brings to you, he is the well himself.

It made me to think over Jesus talking to the wicked woman who had been so wicked all her life, she was a woman that was filled with adultery and that she married one husband after another one. Of course she would not be anything today if she was here, she'd laugh at her 7 husbands being a small beginning.

That well, I drank out of it myself. It's water that is very light and easy to digest in your body and my body, I tried it. Little boys come around serving you with it and they expect you to give them a little something, and so I kept reaching for another cup, I wanted to know whether or not this water was health water and would not have any effect on your body, so I kept drinking cupful after cupful, when I left from them my stomach felt just as light as it did when I came, I said that must be the well you drink out of

The Honorable Mr. Elijah Muhammad

and you don't need to be thirsty because you can drink plenty of that water and it don't lay heavy on your stomach. Of course the spiritual side teaching of the well that never goes dry in the Bible and Holy Qur'an both that it is referring to the spiritual well of God.

PART VIII

The Future Master Fard Muhammad

The Mother Plane

The Mother Plane was made to destroy this world of evil and to show the wisdom and mighty power of the God Whom came to destroy an old world and set up a new world.

The nature of the new world is righteousness. The nature of the new world cannot be righteousness, as long as unrighteousness is in its midst. The same type of Plane was used by the Original God to put mountains on His planets.

Allah (God) Who came in the Person of Master Fard Muhammad, to Whom praises are due forever, is wiser than any god before Him as the Bible and the Holy Qur'an teach us. He taught me that this will be used to raise mountains on this planet (earth). The mountains that He will put on this earth will not be very high. He will raise these mountains to a height of one (1) mile over the United States of America.

This reminds us of the prophet's prediction of this time of the destruction of the old world and the

The Honorable Mr. Elijah Muhammad

bringing in of a new world: "Behold, the Lord, maketh the earth empty, and maketh it waste, and turneth it upside down, and scattereth abroad the inhabitants thereof." (Bible Is. 24:1)

There are planes in various nations today, but this is the mother of them all. Why? Because this type of Plane was used before the making of this world. Why should God make such a sign of His power to destroy a nation? Because this is the final destruction of that people who have opposed God in His purpose and aims for Justice and Righteousness.

The white race is not a people who were made righteous and then turned to unrighteousness; they were made unrighteous by the god who made them (Mr. Yakub).

Allah (God) Who came in the Person of Master Fard Muhammad, to Whom praises are due forever, taught me that this Plane is capable of reaching a height of forty miles above the earth. His words could have been a sign meaning forty years, in which the Plane would go into action and not referring actually to forty miles. Allah (God) does not speak one word that does not have meaning. Every word that He speaks has meaning.

The Mother Plane, according to what has been described of it by the devil scientists, is capable of not only staying up for long periods of time; but it is also capable of eluding the scientists. They want to attack and destroy it; but if a plane did get close enough to attempt to carry out this purpose, it would be destroyed instead. The white man has learned that this is not a place to be played with. Planes come out of the Mother Plane.

In the 1930's Canadian newspapers reported that they saw the wheel (Mother Plane). It came down out of the sky. They admitted that it looked like a great city, and that something came down from it; it appeared to be a tube, but the tube—like thing went back up again.

Allah (God) Who came in the Person of Master Fard Muhammad, to Whom praises are due forever, taught me that after six months to a year, the Mother Plane comes into the gravity of the earth. It takes on oxygen and hydrogen in order to permit it to stay out of the earth's gravity until it needs refueling again.

EZEKIEL'S PROPHECY OF THE WHEEL

Ezekiel saw the Mother Plane in a vision. According to the Bible, he looked up and saw this Plane (Ez. 1:16) and he called it a wheel because it was made like a wheel. A Plane that is wheel—shaped can turn in any direction, at any time.

The Honorable Mr. Elijah Muhammad

He admitted that the Plane was so high that it looked dreadful, and he cried out, "O wheel". *(Ez. 10:13)*

Ezekiel saw great work going on in the wheel and four living creatures "and their work was as it were a wheel in the middle of a wheel." (Ez. 1:16). And when the living creatures went, the wheels went with them: and when the living creatures were lifted up from the earth, the wheels, were lifted up Ez. 1:19. The power of the lifting up of the four creatures was in the wheel. The four creatures represents the four colors of the original people of the earth.

There are five great powers of the nations of the earth. These five Powers are the Black, Brown, Yellow, Red and white. Of the four Original Powers, the Red is not an equal Power. The vision shows the four creatures being lifted up from the earth. When the wheel was lifted up, they were lifted up and when the wheel stood, they stood. This means that they waited upon the movement of the wheel.

In Ezekiel's vision concerning the wheel, he said that he heard the voice of one tell the other to take coals of fire and to scatter it over the cities; this means bombs. It could mean fire too, however. The Plane is to drop bombs which would automatically be timed to burrow quickly to a position of one mile below the surface of the earth where they are timed to explode.

Allah (God) taught me that these bombs are not to be dropped into water. They are to be dropped only

The Future Master Fard Muhammad

on the cities. It will be the work of the wheel. The wheel is the power of the four creatures, namely the four colors of the Black man (Black, brown, yellow and red). The red Indian is to benefit also from the judgment of the world.

We must remember that God comes to separate from the righteous that which is hindering the righteous from making progress and to destroy the effect of the poison of that which has opposed the righteous. The effect of the poison will be fully destroyed after the destruction of the source of the poison, which has poisoned the righteous.

It is like one being bitten by a rattlesnake. Quickly medication is administered in order to minimize the effect of the poison upon flesh and blood until a complete cure is effected; and the patient recuperates and is well again.

It is useless to try to ignore Ezekiel's vision of the wheel, for the make and the destructive work of the wheel was foretold before it came to pass. The disbeliever believes that which he sees present and not that which is prophesied to come. That is why he is the loser and takes the course to hell, because he disbelieves in that which is prophesied to come about a particular day. This is what the enemy is trying to do today with the Black Man. He is fascinating him with sport and play and indecency and the doing of evil to keep him from going to the God Who is present.

The Honorable Mr. Elijah Muhammad

You never thought the day would come when you would see your wife, mother and old grey—haired women walking down the street today, half—nude. A few years ago they would not have dared to come out into the public like that. But now they do so because the devil has put his approval on this kind of attire. They desire to please the devil. They do whatever the devil bids them to do. The devil desires to take the Black man with him to his doom.

Let us not classify the prophets as liars and ignore their prophecies for we may cause our self—destruction through belief in the devil instead of belief in the God of Righteousness. There is no known equal of the Mother Plane. This is the reason why she is called the Mother Plane. The Mother Plane is made for the purpose of destroying the present world. She has no equal. Do not marvel at the make of this plane, since it is from the God Who made the universe of floating planets and stars which are supported only by the Power of Allah in their rotation in their orbits.

Allah (God) Whom came in the Person of Master Fard Muhammad, to Whom praises are due forever, taught me that the Mother plane is a little human—made planet. Is it not simple for Allah (God) to make a new planet if He wants to? The Mother Plane is capable of staying out of the earth's gravity for a whole year. She is capable of producing her own sphere of oxygen and hydrogen, as any other planet is

The Future Master Fard Muhammad

able to do. The Mother Plane carries the same type of bomb on her that our Black scientists dropped on the planet earth to bring up mountains out of the earth after the planet earth was created.

The knowledge of how to do this has not been given to the world (white race), nor will they ever get this kind of knowledge. The knowledge of the world is limited. If the devil would get this type of knowledge we could just say that we are goners. However, they are not able to attain this type of knowledge.

What does a six day old baby (white race) look like trying to compete with a six year old child (Black Nation)? For the six year old child can run all out in the yard and play. He can eat solid food. The power of the six day old baby is limited. The knowledge and power of this world's life (white race) is limited. The world of the white man was made from what he found and what he has seen and learned from the work of the original Black man. The white race is far from being able to equal the power and wisdom of the original Black man.

The Mother Plane and her work is a display of the power of the mightiest God, Master Fard Muhammad, to Whom praises are due forever. Master Fard Muhammad, to Whom praises are due forever, is the Wisest and Best Knower; He is the Mightiest of Them All. "O wheel," says the prophet

The Honorable Mr. Elijah Muhammad

Ezekiel. She was so high up in the sky that she looked dreadful.

She is capable of staying away from you who plan the destruction of her. She is capable of confusing you who would try to reach her with your means of destruction. There are scientists on the Mother Plane who know what you are thinking about before the thought materializes (Holy Qur'an Ch. 50:16). Therefore, it is impossible to try to attack the Mother Plane. She can attack you, but you cannot attack her.

The Mother Plane can hide behind other stars and make herself invisible to the eye because she does not have to wait on a power from the earth. She can produce her own power to go wherever she desires to go in space. The Mother Plane is not like your little bullets or cameras which are powered by your limited power. The Bible prophesies that today Allah (God) wishes to make known to us that He is God. He wishes to be respected as the superior God. He wishes all life in the universe to know that He is the greatest.

The Muslim recognizes Allah (God) to be the greatest. He always repeats "Thou art the greatest. There is no god Like unto Thee, None deserves to be served or worshipped besides thee." O mighty wheel. I repeat, that there is plenty of significance to the make of the Mother Plane. There is much significance to the course of operation of her work.

The Future Master Fard Muhammad

Space here in this book is limited, but what Allah (God) taught me concerning the Mother Plane could be put into book—form.

O wheel, made to rock the earth and to heave up mountains upon the earth. O wheel, destroyer of nations. No wonder the prophet Isaiah prophesied that the "earth shall reel to and fro like a drunkard..." (Bible; Is. 24:20). Let us seek refuge in Allah (God) from the destructive work to come from this Mother of Planes.

Message To The BlackMan

A GUIDE TO UNDERSTANDING THE BIBLE

The Bible referred to unless otherwise noted is the one commonly known as The Authorized (King James) Version.

Subject	Bible	Page
Accepted Guidance of Serpent	Gen 3:6	74
Against friendship with devils	James 4:4	109
Against nature to love your enemies	Luke 6:27-29	96
Against workers of iniquity	Psalms 95:16	10
Agreement broken	Isaiah 29:17-1818	107
America and Negro symbol as Eagle and Carcass	Matt 25:28	300
America compared with Babylon	Jer 51:81	273
America modern Babylon	Eze 14:13	273
America's scientists troubled	Eze 21:15	300
Answer to charges	Luke 15:4,6	96
Be fruitful and multiply	Gen 1:26-28	121
Be not deceived	Deut 11:16	8
Both cast in lake of fire	Rev 19:20	203
Bounds of their habitations	Act 16:31	334
Bowed to golden calf	Exod 32:4	74
Bring you into your own land	Eze 36:24	20
Came from East	Matt 24:27	12
Chastisement as consequence of rejection	Rev 21:8	297
Chastisement as consequence of rejection	Rev 9:6, 19:20	297
Chastisement as consequence of rejection	Rev 20:10,4,15	207
Come out of her	Rev 18:4	88
Coming of God	Habakkuk 3	7
Coming of Son of Man	Matt 24:27	10
Created them in His image	Gen 1:27	121
Creating a race	Gen 1:26	54
Curse of Noah	Gen 9:21-25	88
Dan shalt be a serpent	Gen 49.17	123
Darkness was open	Gen 1.2	95
Day of the Lord	Peter 3:10	281
Day of the Lord is near	Joel 3:14	268
Deceive nations	Thess 2:9	2
Delivered Jonah	Jonah 2:2-4	141
Devil deceived people of paradise	Gen 3:13	128
Devil deceived the woman	Rev 12:4	127
Devil kill own brother	Gen 4:8	128
Devils seek to slay the Negroes	Psalms 37:32	274
Don't try to master heaven and earth	Isaiah 14:13	110
Don't try to master heaven and earth	Isaiah 14:16	110
Enemy sentenced to death	Rev 20:10-14	272

GUIDE TO UNDERSTANDING THE BIBLE

Everlasting life	John 8:12	330
Every Heart shall melt	Eze 21:7	300
Fall of America	Rev 18:2	276
Fear God Who has power	Rev 21:8	30
Fear of Man	Pro 29:25	29
Fearful and unbelieving	Rev 21:8	99
Fed and sheltered Israel in desert	Exod 16:12-15	101
First parents of white race	Gen 3:20-24	133
Flesh and blood cannot enter heaven	Cor 15:50	12
Garden of Paradise	Gen 3:1	127
Gentiles prepare war	Joel 3:9	268
God pleads with you to get out of America	Rev 18:4	272
God's power	Habakkuk 3:4	7
Great deceiver	Rev 20:3-8	83
He departed from evil maketh himself a prey	Isaiah 59:15	324
He was sent	John 4:34	27
He was sent	Matt 15:24	27
Holy One from Mount Paran	Habakkuk 3:3	7
I. the Lord, Thy Saviour	Isaiah 49:24-26	299
If God was your father	John 8:42	23
In the beginning	Gen 1:1	94
Innocent earth's blood	Gen 4:10	128
Jehovah calls Moses	Exo 3:4	86
Knoweth no man	Matt 24:36	11
Lazarus	St. Luke 16 & St. John 11	25
Let us make man	Gen 1:26	95-118
Loosening of Devil	Rev 20:7	3
Loosening of Devil	Rev 20:308-10	2
Lost Sheep (People)	Luke 15:11	297
Lost Sheep, Prodigal Son	Luke 15:21-22	95
Love one another	John 15:17	33
Love the brotherhood	I Peter 2:17	33
Make all things new	Rev. 21:5	82
Moses call Dan a Lion's whelp	Deut 33:22	123
Nations set for showdown	Joel 2:2	270
Neither is there salvation	Acts 4:12	330
No other God	Isaiah 45:22	27
No other God	Marks 12:32	27
No other God	Isaiah 46:9	27
Not know God by His name	Exod 6:3	21
144,000 return to God	Rev 14:1	46
People spiritually as beast	Rev 12 & 13	47
Prodigal Son	St. Luke 15:11	25
Prophecy of lost people	Gen 15:13	250

GUIDE TO UNDERSTANDING THE BIBLE

Prophet raised from brethren	Deut 18:18	250
Race of Devils	I Cor 10:21	338
Race of devils	Rev 12:9-17	106
Race of devils	2 Thess 2:3-12	106
Race of devils	2 Thess 2:3,4, 7-12	338
Race of devils	John 8:44	338
Redemption of so-called Negro	Deut 18:15,18	278
Redemption of so-called Negro	Matt 25:32	278
Redemption of so-called Negro	Rev 14	278
Religion of Peace	2 Thess 3:16	69
Religion of Peace	Psalms 35:8	69
Religion of Peace	Psalms 29:11	69
Rest from fear	Isaiah 14:3	29
Sacrifice sons and daughters unto devils	Psalms 106:37	32
Same in last judgment	Matt 24:37-39	11
Saw God as material being	Habakkuk 3:3	7
Saw God coming	I Cor 1:36	7
Seek kingdom of heaven	Luke 12:31	155
Serpent as a deceiver	Rev 12:9	127
Shall never hunger	John 6:35	330
Shall not live by bread alone	Matt 4:4	155
Should not worship up devils	Rev 9:20	232
Showdown between forces of world and Allah	Joel 3:2,3	268
Signs of God's coming	Matt 24	286
So-called Negro and his enemy	Joel 3:7	268
Son of Man	2 Thess 2:8-9	14
Son of Man coming	Matt 24:30	18
Swine forbidden	Deut 14:8	247
Teman, a son of Esau	Gen 36:11,15,42	7
Ten Commandments	Exod 20:1-18	90
The land of Egypt	Exod 16:2,3,8	155
The old serpent called devil and satan	Rev 12:9	122
The throne of iniquity	Psalms 94:20	131
Thee of good and evil	Gen 2:17	126
They love their master	Jer 2:14	232
Thou forsaken men	Matt 27:46	7
Thou shall be saved	Acts 16:31	330
Thy people	Habakkuk 3:13	8
To be destroyed	Rev 19:20	88
To be destroyed	Dan 7:11,19	88
	(or HQ?)	97
Truth make you free	John 8:32	
Under name of Israel	2 Chron 6:31-39	138
Weapons no good against Allah	Rev 16:6	128

GUIDE TO UNDERSTANDING THE BIBLE

Who is able to make war	Dan 7:7	126
Who is like unto the beast?	Rev 13:4	124-126
Wicked watches the righteous	Psalms 37:32	10
Work of god against enemy	Habakkuk 3	7
Worship white man as God	Rev 14:4	263
Ye have condemned and killed the just	James 5:6	258
You should not have fellowship with devils	I Cor 20:21	232

GUIDE TO UNDERSTANDING THE HOLY QURAN

The Holy Qur'an referred to unless otherwise noted is the Arabic Text, translation and commentary (Revised Edition) BY Maulana Muhammad Ali. 3rd or 4th Edition.

Subject	Holy Qur'an	Page
A flame lying in wait for him	72:8-9	110
A Muslim is not a Muslim unless	30:30	79-80
Abode of peace	10:25	70
All Messengers attacked by disbelievers and government of their time	13:32	188
Allah, Best Knower	2:1	21
Allah does not have him who is treacherous	4:107	255
Allah does not love disbelievers	3:31	259
Allah does not spare oppressors to Messengers	66:1-11	266
Allah is One	112:1	73
Allah knows what's in our hearts		136
Allah, The Mighty, Knowing	40:2	92
Allah will gather hypocrites, disbelievers	4:140,142,145 (138-178?)	260
Allah will pay back the hypocrite	2:15	252
Allah will perfect His light	61:8	76
Allah will not forgive those who hinder	47: 33-34	260
America in for trouble	44:10	303
Be steadfast in prayer	4:103	143
Be steadfast in the Cause of Allah		135
Best remembrance of Allah through prayer		136
Beware of hypocrites	68:10-16	269
Black mud fashioned into shape	15:28	128
Celebrate the praise of Lord	20:130	143
Chosen for your, Islam	5:3	69
Corruption has appeared in the Land	30:41	265
Created man from sperm	76:2	119
Days of Allah	45:14	22
Deceive only themselves	2:8	255
Devil called serpent	37:65	126
Devil came upon them from before them	7:17	104

GUIDE TO UNDERSTANDING THE HOLY QUR'AN

Devil deserts man	25:29	296
Devil is your open enemy	2:208	149
Devil respite me	7:14	134
Devil swear to be sincere adviser	7:21	105
Devil's time limited	2:36	133
Devil with blue eyes	20:102	13
Dominate other religion	61:8,9	71
Do not act hostile to Messenger	4:115	260
Encompasses all things	7:156	73
Enter into submission	2:208	149
Fear Allah	2:2	86
Fear Allah	7:18	30
Fear Allah	15:43	30
Fill hell with you all	7:18	303
Fill hell with you all	7:18	105
Follow right direction	32:3	22
Forgiveness and a great reward	8:10	136
Gave Book to Moses	32:23	87
Givers of good news and as warners	4:163-165	132
Glorify Allah	30:17	143
Grievous chastisement	2:7	255
He forgives whom He pleases	2:284	160
He it is Who sent His Apostle	61:9	75
Hear and obey	2:285	98
Hypocrites along with the devils	2:14	255
Hypocrites are dishonest	2:16	255
Hypocrites are liars	63:1	252
Hypocrites are warned	4:109	260
Hypocrites practice deceit	47:23-25	254
Hypocrites ruin only themselves	4:113	256
Hypocrites seek friends with enemy of Islam	5:53	253
Hypocrites seek to deceive believers	2:9	252
Hypocrites seek to slander	104	254
Hypocrites warned against trying to deceive	4:150	253
I will lie in wait	7:16	134
In the Name of Allah		141
In their hearts a disease	2:10	255
Keep your duty to Me	2:40-41	99
Let not the devil seduce you	7:27	101
Lord of the Worlds	32:1-2	87
Make me to keep up prayer		136
Make not mischief	2:11	255
Meaning of Mahdi	22:54	294
Messenger believes what revealed to him	2:285	259
Messenger warned not to be easy on hypocrites	66:10	254

GUIDE TO UNDERSTANDING THE HOLY QUR'AN

Mix not up the truth	2:42	98
My religion	10:104	81
No fear for Him	2:112	70
No good in their secret counsel	4:114	256
No help for hypocrites	4:144-145	253
None dispute Message but those who disbelieve	40:4	206
None other than Islam	4:163	13
Nor shall they grieve	2:62	132
O mankind, surely we created you	49:13	118
Obey Allah and Messenger	3:31	259
Observe prayers	17:78-79	143
One who shall rule	2:30	128
Pardons most through His Messenger		136
Patience and prayer	2:45	143
People of Noah reject Messenger	40:5	208
Perfected for you	5:3	80
Planners of evil for the Messenger	8:46	256
Possessor of power over all things	2:284	160
Prayer is better than sleep	33:41-43	137
Prayer keeps one away from evil	29:45	135
Prayers are good deeds	11:114	143
Prophet, sent you as a witness	33:45-46	137
Punishment sure to overtake hypocrites	9:63	263
Religion of Allah, Islam	30:30	71
Remember Allah's Favor upon you		135
Remembrance of Allah is greatest force	29:45	135
Return to your land	89:27-30	305
Reward for those believers in Allah and His Messenger	4:152	253
Right religion	30:43	78
Scripture same as revealed	4:163-164	93
Shun the devil	16:36	132
Strive hard against disbelievers and hypocrites	9:73-74	256
Submit to Allah	2:112	29
Submit to Allah	3:82	77
Take not Jews and Christians for friends	5:51	160
They plan but against themselves	6:124	256
They will be separated	30:43	143
This Book no doubt	2:2	86
Those against Messenger enters hell	4:115	256
Those who disbelieve	2:6	255
Took devils for friends	7:30	105
True religion	3:18	77
True religion with Allah	3:18	69-71
Turned into apes and swine	18:	103

GUIDE TO UNDERSTANDING THE HOLY QUR'AN

Victory over disbelievers	2:286	160
Warn a people whom no warner has come before		249-251
We hear and obey	2:285	160
Who will contend with Allah	4:109	256
Wish not to have taken devil for friend	25:28	296
Woe, woe to America	45:28-29	300
Works of devil	7:14-18	13
Worship no God but Allah	1:12	75
Would I had taken with the Messenger	25:27	204
Your God is One God	18:110	27

COMING SOON BY:
ALI MAHDI MUHAMMAD:

Knowledge of The Gods

Al Fard

Seven Steps to Allah God

English Lesson C-2

AVAILABLE NOW

Uncle Yah Yah $14.95

Uncle Yah Yah Pt 2 $19.95 (Hardcover)

S/H $4.25 for one book $7.00 for both

New World Nation of Islam
PO Box 8466
Newark, NJ 07108
www.newworldnationislam.com

email your sales questions to:
admin-orders@newworldnationislam.com

New World Nation of Islam
Order Form

Please Print:

Name:_____

Address:_____

City/State:_____

Zip:_____

RUSH: _____ copy/copies of **The Future Master Fard Muhammad** by The Honorable Elijah Muhammad **$12.95**

RUSH: _____ copy/copies of Uncle Yah Yah :21st Century Man of Wisdom by Al Dickens **$14.95**

RUSH: _____ copy/copies of Uncle Yah Yah: 21st Century Man of Wisdom **Part 2** by Al Dickens **$19.95**

Shipping/Handling: **$4.25 per book $2.75 ea/additional book**

Total Amount enclosed $_____

Make **MONEY ORDERS & CHECKS** Payable to:

New World Nation of Islam
P.O. Box 8466
Newark, NJ 07108
admin-orders@newworldnationislam.com

Please allow 10-14 Business days for delivery.
Books are shipped via Media Mail.
www.newworldnationislam.com